Composition, Creative Writing Studies, and the Digital Humanities

Also available from Bloomsbury

The Bloomsbury Introduction to Creative Writing,
Tara Mokhtari
Creative Writing in the Community: A Guide,
Terry Ann Thaxton
Creative Writing in a Digital Age,
Michael Dean Clark, Trent Hergenrader and Joseph Rein

Composition, Creative Writing Studies, and the Digital Humanities

Adam Koehler

BLOOMSBURY ACADEMIC
LONDON • NEW YORK • OXFORD • NEW DELHI • SYDNEY

BLOOMSBURY ACADEMIC
Bloomsbury Publishing Plc
50 Bedford Square, London, WC1B 3DP, UK
1385 Broadway, New York, NY 10018, USA

BLOOMSBURY, BLOOMSBURY ACADEMIC and the Diana logo are
trademarks of Bloomsbury Publishing Plc

First published in Great Britain 2017
Paperback edition first published 2018

Cover design: Simon Levy
Cover image © iStock

A catalogue record for this book is available from the British Library.

ISBN: HB: 978-1-4725-9194-4
PB: 978-1-3501-0298-9
ePDF: 978-1-4725-9196-8
ePub: 978-1-4725-9195-1

A catalog record for this book is available from the Library of Congress.

Typeset by Deanta Global Publishing Services, Chennai, India

To find out more about our authors and books visit
www.bloomsbury.com and sign up for our newsletters.

For Stephanie,
electric in all the best ways

Contents

Acknowledgments   viii

Foreword, *Tim Mayers*   xi

Introduction   1

1   Digital Pasts: On Composition, Creative Writing, and
Emergent Technologies   23

2   Defining Digital Creative Writing Studies   45

3   Ideology, Subjectivity, and the Creative Writer in the Digital Age   69

4   Process, Genre, and Technologizing the Word   95

5   Fenceless Neighbors: On Composition, Creative Writing, and
Emerging Institutional Practices   119

Works Cited   139

Index   145

Acknowledgments

This book is the result of support from several people I'm fortunate enough to call teachers, colleagues, friends, and family. The unparalleled mentorship of Jeanne Colleran, Maryclaire Moroney, Tom Pace, Tom Hayes, Francis Ryan, and Brian Macaskill exemplified the sort of dynamism and rigor that led directly to this book. They introduced me to vital sets of areas within the discipline of English studies and, perhaps more importantly, let me combine and play with them. Their teaching and willingness to experiment have been foundational for me.

At the University of Wisconsin—Madison, the leadership of Mike Bernard-Donals, Judy Mitchell, Deb Brandt, Marty Nystrand, Ron Kuka, David Fleming, Amaud Johnson, Brad Hughes, Lorrie Moore, and Rob Nixon showed me exactly the kind of mixed cocktail studying composition and creative writing could be. I am more grateful than I can express here. And to my graduate school colleagues—Scot Barnett, Annette Vee, Kate Viera, Rik Hunter, Jacque Preston, Eric Pritchard, Mary Fiorenza, Mira Shimabukuro, David Grant, and Alice Dear—you showed me first what it means to love what you do and to make a life out of it. Thank you. And especially to Tim Laquintano who helped me turn an idea talked about late at night on his porch into the book you're holding now and to Corey Mead and Laura Sims, whose friendships (independently and together) have saved me more times than I care to admit.

This book simply wouldn't exist without the considerable support of Tim Mayers. His willingness to respond to emails from an eager reader and to suggest readings and thinkers has deeply shaped the argument in this book. I am considerably grateful for his professionalism, creativity, and critical reading. I am also deeply in debt to Geoff Sirc and Jeff Rice, who both provided perspective on this project when I needed it most; to Bryon Hawk who showed me what book proposals were supposed to look like; to Thomas Rickert whose perspective on a version of these ideas early on in my career was, excuse the pun, instrumental; to Kelly Ritter, whose editorial work at *College English* planted the seed that would eventually become this book's argument; to Trent

Hergenrader, Michael Clark, and Joseph Rein, who showed me that more than two people would care about this argument; to Dan Collins, Derek Owens, Roseanne Gatto, and Tara Roeder, who are the world's best conference buddies. To all of you who welcomed me into the field and challenged my work and asked good questions at panels: thank you.

This book is also indebted to a small literary magazine I cofounded on a very cold night at a top-class Chinese restaurant in Madison, Wisconsin. Thank you to my *Avery* family and the authors who were brave enough to let a new literary magazine publish their work: coeditors Andrew Palmer, Stephanie Fiorelli, Emma Fusco-Straub, Nicolette Kittinger, and Michael Fusco-Straub. A special thank you to Kevin Brockmeier and Junot Diaz, who each served as judges for our Small Spaces Short Fiction Prize. You all made soliciting submissions, attending book festivals, and talking to one's literary heroes even more extraordinary than it already is. And to those who supported *Avery* without thinking twice—Frank Bures, Rae Meadows, Dave Eggers, and Jason Daley—whose generosity and belief in the work of the writer may seem only natural to them. But to me it is heroic. It makes my heart swell.

Thanks also to David Avital, Mark Richardson, and everyone at Bloomsbury for their assistance and support. Their passion for finding new waves of research and for taking risks vital to the field as it continually develops has been inspiring. Thanks also to the anonymous reviewers who provided excellent comments and insight into the manuscript.

And to my colleagues at Manhattan College and elsewhere—David Witzling, Rocco Marinaccio, Ashley Cross, Patrick Horner, Deirdre O'Leary, Heidi Laudien, Meg Toth, Brian Chalk, Bridget Chalk, Maeve Adams, Dominika Wrozynski, Suzanne Cope, Suzanne Barnett, Zach Snider, James Arnett, Kelly Marin, Cory Blad, Mehnaz Afridi, Paul Droubie, and Natalia Imperatori-Lee—thank you for your humor, collegiality, and friendship. They help me see what being a professional day in and day out is all about.

To those friends who were there first and have been counted on ever since: Eric Long, John Rachel, Ari Vigil. I love you.

Thank you to my parents, Carol and Rick Koehler, who will claim not to understand a word in this book, but who will support it anyway. Their unconditional love and encouragement has prepared me for a life of writing in ways they never could have anticipated. To Kevin and Paly Koehler, David and Mary Catherine Koehler, and Annie and George Koehler: the world has never known a more warm-hearted and beautiful crew. (It's been scientifically proven.) And a very special thank you to Connie and Billy Fiorelli, Lindsey Fiorelli, and Jordan Rodu for being the kind of family that is outrageous and kind enough to make one want to self-select into it.

But most importantly I am indebted to my first and most ravenous reader: Stephanie. Her insight and critical acumen and vitality electrify my work and my life. And to our children, Sebastian and Mia, who remind me to try out new and possibly dangerous ideas every day. To them I owe the greatest thanks.

Foreword

Tim Mayers

Sometimes things are most difficult to see when they are right in front of you. And sometimes, if the things themselves seem clear, the nature of the *connections between them* is difficult, if not nearly impossible, to see. I am delighted to be writing these words of introduction for Adam Koehler's book because of the connections I believe this book will allow us to see (or, if we have already seen them, that it will help us to articulate). This book will, along with much other exciting scholarship in *creative writing studies* published during the second decade of the twenty-first century, help establish and clarify the terms of a scholarly conversation that will—and must—continue into the coming years.

Writing, certainly one of the most consequential inventions in human history, serves as a great example of how we can miss what should be most obvious. Writing is so much a part of our hyper-literate society that we usually can't see it in anything approaching its fullness. Nor can we often see writing's connections, in their fullness, to virtually everything else in our lives. Discussions of writing in the public sphere, and in parts of academia (especially the composition classroom) often get bogged down in complaints about comma splices or text-message abbreviations or a host of other perceived errors. In creative writing workshops, concerns about static surface features of individual pieces of writing can also have a tendency to overshadow much more consequential matters. All the tiny details—the minutiae—too often blind us to the breathtaking and dynamic scope of all that writing is, and can be.

Surely some of that difficulty arises because the word "writing" is used in at least several different senses. Many of the key words of our culture(s) present a similar difficulty. In an ambitious recent work entitled *The Nature of Technology: What It is and How It Evolves*, W. Brian Arthur writes, "'Technology' has at least half-a-dozen major meanings, and several of these conflict." Words closely associated or overlapping with "technology," he continues, are "loaded with emotional associations" (5). A major theme of Arthur's book is that, in spite of the saturation of the human lifeworld by technologies of numerous sorts, we don't really yet have "an '-ology' of Technology. . . . We have no agreement on what the word 'technology' means, no overall theory of how technology came into being . . . no deep understanding of what 'innovation' consists of, and no theory of evolution for technology" (12–13). How ironic it is, then—but also how *telling*—that in Arthur's otherwise fascinating book, he mentions *writing* almost not at all, and *language* only in passing on a few occasions. He seems to have missed the possibility that writing could be a foundational technology that makes so many other technologies possible. He seems to have missed the possibility that without writing, virtually all of the recent "advances" in engineering and the sciences would be unimaginable. *As a technology*, writing fades into invisibility for Arthur, even while he is . . . well, *writing*!

Another thing often easy to miss is this: scholarly writing, in its idealized sense, is supposed to constitute a type of "conversation" (think of the Burkean metaphor of the parlor, so ritually cited in so many places by now that it's become its own sort of cliché). The scholarly conversation is supposed to advance and extend knowledge—or to explore questions—in ways that no single individual can; the conversation, by its nature, is supposed to be bigger and more important than any individual participant. And yet how often are our parts in these conversations distorted by the necessity of considering them as mere lines on *curriculum vitae* or items on pages of works cited? Even worse, how often do our parts in scholarly conversations go unanswered or unacknowledged? In light of these questions, I feel both fortunate and honored that this book not only cites some of my work but also challenges it and extends it. Koehler's reading, in Chapter 1, of the overlapping and problematic histories of how "the creative" has figured in composition scholarship over the past half century often had me nodding in agreement, pausing to ponder its implications, and making notes for future reading. Adam Koehler situates my scholarly work (and the work of many others) in a way that I could not have done so myself; he helps me better understand the place of my own work—and the work of others—in the larger conversation. In his later chapters, Koehler builds upon this insightful reading of disciplinary and subdisciplinary history to show how something called *digital creative writing studies* is not only a possibility for the future (a future in which it might help English studies survive by renegotiating calcified terms and ideas that would keep it stuck in the past), but something that is being practiced right now, something we can find if we know how to look for it, and something that has roots reaching decades into the past, again if we know how to look for it.

When I was a graduate student from the mid- to late-1990s, I was deeply at work on a doctoral dissertation on the past, present, and potential future relationships between composition studies and creative writing (a topic that continues to consume much of my scholarly attention even now, two decades later). But I was also deeply involved in a then relatively new subfield of composition studies called "computers and writing." I was teaching composition in a networked classroom with a computer station for each student, experimenting with class discussions in chat-room environments, and engaging in (almost) real-time scholarly conversations via e-mail listservs. I had a vague sense then that these two facets of my emerging professional life connected somehow—or at least *ought to have* connected somehow. But it was difficult to articulate those connections, and in the ensuing years I never succeeded in doing so, beyond a few broad gestures. But now, with the publication of this book by Adam Koehler, in which he identifies and maps out the domain of *digital creative writing studies*, those connections become much clearer.

Perhaps twenty or thirty years from now, it will seem odd—a distinct historical curiosity—that we ever drew such sharp (even if usually implicit) lines of demarcation between "composition," "creative writing," and "technology." The pace of technological change with regard to writing has, until recently, been slow enough to allow practices and ideas to become established as apparently "natural." Writing existed for thousands of years before the widespread adoption of print technology, which itself held primary sway for a much shorter period of time (a couple of centuries, give or take a decade or two). The word processor as a writing tool (and the computer on which it usually operates as software) has been in widespread use only since the 1980s, and already many of the earliest word processing programs are essentially obsolete. The smart phone was not introduced to the market until the first decade of the twenty-first century, and already it operates as a daily writing tool for many people. There is no reason to expect that this pace of technological change will slow down any time soon. Today's common writing tools (including the state-of-the-art Mac laptop on which I am composing this foreword) are likely to seem obsolete a decade from now, if not sooner. Older writing tools will almost certainly mingle with the new, but the overall landscape of writing will have changed.

In that kind of environment, what will "creative writing" look like? How will the literary and generic forms inherited from the age of print have evolved in new composing and reading environments? How might these developments have affected the teaching of writing? This book you are about to read will help prepare you for the possibilities.

Introduction

In *Composition, Creative Writing Studies, and the Digital Humanities* I critically examine how scholarship and pedagogy in the fields of composition studies and creative writing have inflected each other at the end of the twentieth and beginning of the twenty-first century, specifically arguing for a distinct and critical extension of creative writing studies that examines the ways in which the act of writing imaginative texts is technologically mediated. Scholars in both composition studies and creative writing such as Wendy Bishop, Paul Kameen, Patrick Bizzaro, Tim Mayers, Paul Dawson, Kelly Ritter, Stephanie Vanderslice, Dianne Donnelly, Katherine Haake, Graeme Harper, and Douglas Hesse, among others, have contributed over the past twenty years to a growing body of scholarship that works within or at the intersection of composition studies and creative writing, each searching in different ways for how research within and between these two areas can reinvigorate work in both fields. This book begins by way of an examination of the variety of disciplinary challenges—calls to unify and/or delineate the disciplines, pedagogical imperatives, theoretical orientations—in order to further refine the relationship between these two fields (rather than revolutionize their place[s] in the institution), then moves to an examination of the ways in which the digital humanities has been called upon in emerging scholarship that seeks to refine, reflect on, and in some senses revise that relationship. At the end of the twentieth and beginning of the twenty-first centuries, as this book will demonstrate, while composition is still trying to figure out its relationship to creative writing and while creative writing is adapting to the moniker "creative writing studies," we see a set of urgent questions emerge: What theoretical and pedagogical innovations have they offered each other? What institutional boundaries should they draw around themselves? How has each field's branching into and theorizing about digital writing affected the other? In short, this book investigates answers to these questions. Or, in the words of Douglas Hesse, "because the new media offer a complex (if not altogether neutral) turf to which we might bring our different traditions [in order to explore] more commonalities even as we respect our dissimilar orientations and aspirations," this book begins the work of critically examining how digital multimodality would work in the context of that shared space between composition studies and creative writing ("The Place of Creative Writing" 49).

I point out three threads of scholarship in order to stage that discussion: (1) scholarship in composition studies that recruits "creative" or aesthetic theories, but that does not explicitly comment on or call upon its relationship with creative writing as a discipline; (2) scholarship that explicitly comments or calls upon the relationship between composition studies and creative writing, often scholars with interests in either exploring institutional borders and/or theoretical and pedagogical points of contact; and (3) emerging scholarship in creative writing studies that examines, as Graeme Harper and Jeri Kroll point out in *Creative Writing Studies: Practice, Research, and Pedagogy*, the ways the field "further invents" itself and "encourages multiple meanings" (xii). Put simply, this book unthreads these three strands of scholarship in order to braid them back together as each has begun to reconstitute itself in an age of the digital humanities.

Aesthetics and "creative composition"

As composition studies went through its infamous institutionalization during the 1960s and 1970s (during which it sometimes glanced askance at its neighbor creative writing in order to situate its place in that institutionalization), scholars recruited aesthetics often associated with "creative" types of writing (collage, memoir, freewriting) in the expressivist theories of that time (Murray, Macrorie); then again in the neo-expressivist scholarship of the 1990s and into the twenty-first century (Sirc, Owens). Derek Owens' *Resisting Writings (and the Boundaries of Composition)* and Geoffrey Sirc's *English Composition as a Happening*, for example, demonstrate how aesthetics and "creative" assignments work across a variety of literacy and power dynamics within the university, ultimately championing a way of imagining writing that invites what they see as marginalized voices into the field of composition. Such arguments, which incorporated a range of aesthetic theory into the teaching of composition, often asked composition scholars to imagine their students as writers or artists. As Ken Macrorie puts it in his book *Telling Writing*:

> This is the first requirement for good writing: truth; not *the* truth (whoever knows surely what that is?), but some kind of truth—a connection between the things written about, the words used in the writing, and the author's experience in a world she knows well—whether in fact or in dream or in imagination. (300)

This notion of writing, prevalent across many other expressivist arguments, is invested in two important points: (1) a will toward a kind of knowing that is not necessarily "academic" in the disciplinary sense—a kind of knowing rooted in an author's experience as much as any critical treatment of "things written about" and therefore a kind of knowing that carries with it a nascent possibility for reinventing what counts as "good" writing in the university by redefining the work "academic" writing is to do (i.e., "creative" work can "count" as much as conventionally "critical" work does in the writing classroom) and (2) that truth is generated from a range of rhetorical circumstances, including the imagination. While expressivism didn't explicitly call for scholarly connections to creative writing as a discipline, it did recruit theories and pedagogies that have been called "creative" or "unconventional" or "experimental" (Sullivan) in the academic space of the composition classroom; as expressivist pedagogies entered composition classrooms, in other words, students wrote personal narratives, collages, free verse. The "creativity" inherent in such writing, so the arguments go, provides students the opportunity to examine voice, form, and meaning in powerful ways. In fact, for scholars like Peter Elbow this devotion to unconventional writing in the composition classroom comes with it important power dynamics for the student in the university. For Elbow (and many others), such assignments open up the opportunity for students to participate in marginalized discourses often overlooked in the sociopolitical space of "academic" writing. Working through issues of individual voice, in other words, as they come to be contextualized—sometimes in problematic ways—by disciplinary discourses, serves the individual student's literacy in a way that helps her cultivate powerful and meaningful texts in a complex rhetorical environment. As a result, expressivists and neoexpressivists often advance arguments that students should be imagined as active writers (sometimes *rather* than students) and assignments should provide space for and help students contextualize a range of individual acts of expression. Aesthetics—the function, value, and ideologies associated with art as well as the deeper consideration for style and poetics—provided several compositionists with the theoretical framework to do so. Along these lines, this thread of composition scholarship argued collectively for a stronger place for "creative" assignments (understood as less formal and/or unconventional kinds of writing) and theories, emphasizing that they be practiced at the service of empowering and enhancing student writing, while nodding toward the possibility that even in some cases, as for Macrorie or Sirc, they could possibly reinvent the field of composition.

That thread of scholarship made a digital turn at the end of the twentieth century. As digital tools and networked environments made composing practices richer and more complex, compositionists mounted arguments for not only employing those tools, but theorizing them into the scene of composition. As Cynthia Selfe explains in her 1998 chair's address for the Conference on College Composition and Communication, "Technology and Literacy: A Story About the Perils of Not Paying Attention:"

> Allowing ourselves the luxury of ignoring technology . . . is not only misguided at the end of the 20th century, it is dangerously shortsighted. And I do not mean, simply, that we are all—each of us—now teaching students who must know how to communicate as informed thinkers and citizens in an increasingly technological world—although this is surely so. This recognition has led composition faculty only to the point of using computers—or having students do so—but not to the point of thinking about what we are doing and understanding at least some of the important implications of our actions. (1166)

That Sirc and Selfe, along with Anne Wysocki and Johndan Johnson-Eilola, collaborated on the book *Writing New Media: Theory and Applications for Expanding the Teaching of Composition*, which addresses the rhetorical and theoretical opportunities for composition scholar-teachers working in/with new media, is no surprise. The field was ready for considering the material reality of working with writers whose primary scene of writing required, as Selfe points out, the use of a computer. The field was populated with journals like *Computers and Composition, Kairos: A Journal of Rhetoric, Technology, and Pedagogy*, and *Enculturation: A Journal of Rhetoric, Writing, and Culture*, which saw the publication of a wealth of research committed to understanding what it means to write in the midst of such rapidly changing media and scene(s) of writing. Visual rhetoric, multimodal composition, and multiliteracy began to take prominence in the discourse. Collin Brooke's *Lingua Fracta*, Byron Hawk's *A Counter-History of Composition*, and Alexander Reid's *The Two Virtuals* all approached writing through networked and electronic environments. And the "Florida School," informed by Gregory Ulmer's concept of electracy, a literacy that emerges from electronic spaces and encompasses a wide range of literate practices and networked ways of knowing, influenced a whole new generation of scholarship. As Jeff Rice points out in *The Rhetoric of Cool: Composition Studies and New Media*, this turn is the product of decades of cultural shifts that amount to a new scene of writing, one that acknowledges that writing is inherently multimodal and networked. For Rice, this new scene of writing requires a kind of literacy distinct from print-based approaches to understanding literacy:

> I look beyond the canonical texts that we believe have shaped our discipline in order to draw upon areas not normally considered relevant to composition studies, but which I find pose long-term possibilities toward inventing new media-based writing practices. My decision to do so is not eccentric; rather I recognize that rhetoric and rhetorical invention emerge out of a number of influences: art, film, literature, music, record covers, cultural studies, imagery, technology, and, of course, writing. Our challenge is to foreground that acknowledgement, not resist it because of its unfamiliarity or because it doesn't fit what we assume writing should entail. (10)

To foreground that acknowledgment is to identify that the spaces afforded writers in digital environments provide important alternative avenues for literacy and expression, avenues that are closed off in "conventional" academic discourse, which, as the expressivist argument goes, often masks oppressive discourses. In Patricia Suzanne Sullivan's words, these arguments "suggest that especially through the use of new technologies, students may be better allowed to express their individual experiences, articulate marginal or underrepresented social realities, as well as critique the limits of dominant sociopolitical discourses and the institutions that perpetuate these discourses" (147).

In other words, first composition got "creative." Then it went digital.

These arguments are primarily interested in composition as a site where students encounter their own literacy in rigorous investigations of process and product that are always geared toward a critical understanding of their own writing and status as writers. While there are several scholars who explore the space between composition studies and creative writing also publishing at this time, the above lineage of scholarship has remained largely indifferent to that relationship.[1] Their conclusions, by contrast, are aimed at developing student literacies at one end (Rice, Selfe, Yancey) and student art at the other (Sirc, Owens)—rather than producing professional working poets or novelists. Yet their work, through recruiting theories and pedagogies of alternative invention and/in multiple discourses, ask scholars and teachers to consider space for what Douglas Hesse has called "creative composing." One of the questions propelling this book stems from the possibilities nested within such a term: What has "creative composition's" digital turn meant for the relationship between composition studies and creative writing? This book is an extended examination of such inflections and how digital multimodality, perhaps more visible in composition than creative writing studies, provides the exigency to examine the growing amount of hybrid research fusing composition studies and creative writing as each field advances deeper into the twenty-first century.

Creative writing and composition

Douglas Hesse's term "creative composition" comes from his 2010 essay in *College Composition and Communication*, "The Place of Creative Writing in Composition." In that essay, Hesse describes what a few decades of scholarship in composition has examined in relation to creative writing as a discipline. Ways of importing pedagogical methods, readings, and even concerns regarding student subjectivities have, he points out, amounted to a collective argument for making critical space for the productive methods of "creative" or "unconventional" writing assignments in the composition classroom. Hesse's argument—thorough, strong, and correctly pointing to the need for these two fields to further address what they have to offer each other—poses the questions: How can we (compositionists) find room for creative writing in what we do? What can we learn from creative writing? Five years later, in 2015, Alexandria Peary and Tom C. Hunley address the other side of that coin in their edited collection *Creative Writing Pedagogies for the Twenty-first Century*, explaining that emerging creative writing scholarship has expressed strong interest in what composition studies can bring to creative writing:

> The examination of existent composition pedagogies is one stage in the continuing evolution of creative writing studies: the next step would be for the field [creative writing] to use these established pedagogies to initiate brand-new ones—as composition studies has done in a flurry over the past thirty-five years. (3)

Creative Writing Pedagogies for the Twenty-first Century, in fact, is modeled after Gary Tate, Amy Rupiper, and Kurt Schick's very influential collection *A Guide to Composition Pedagogies*, published in 2001. Peary and Hunley's book, in other words, is complementary insofar as that collection works toward shaping pedagogies for creative writing beyond the workshop model by recruiting work done in composition studies over the last thirty-five years.

It's no accident that *Creative Writing Pedagogies for the Twenty-first Century* is dedicated to Wendy Bishop. Bishop works easily as a starting point for examining the relationship between composition and creative writing; her pioneering career within and between both fields contributed largely to a discussion that would grow to include scholars Patrick Bizzaro, Katherine Haake, Kelly Ritter, Stephanie Vanderslice, Paul Kameen, and Tim Mayers, each of whom have continued to develop the relationship that Bishop redefined. I say "redefined" because, as D. G. Myers points out in *The Elephants Teach: Creative Writing Since 1880*, although Bishop was a pioneer when it came to research that examined the space between composition and creative writing, these two fields share a long and complex history—and early in the nineteenth century exhibited little to no disciplinary differences. As Myers famously points out, the first creative writing classes in higher education were Harvard's "Advanced Composition" courses, which, as composition studies began to define itself along the lines of a narrower understanding of "literacy" (academic and disciplinary), eventually saw creative writing unhinge itself from composition in order to follow a separate disciplinary path. Hesse points out in his essay, "The Place of Creative Writing in Composition," that despite a few articles citing the value of using imaginative literature in the composition classroom, not much was made out of the potential relationship between composition and creative writing until the late twentieth century, much of which was initiated by the work of Wendy Bishop.

Bishop's work helped create the shared space between creative writing and composition to which this book aims to contribute. Her collection of essays, edited with Hans Ostrom, *Colors of a Different Horse: Rethinking Creative Writing Theory and Pedagogy* and *Keywords in Creative Writing* (coedited with David Starkey), along with work like Joseph Moxley's edited collection *Creative Writing in America: Theory and Pedagogy*, now stands as a foundational text in an area of writing studies that urges scholars to work across the interdisciplinary space of composition studies and creative writing. Kelly Ritter and Stephanie Vanderslice's edited collection *Can It Really Be Taught? Resisting Lore in Creative Writing Pedagogy* extends these concerns beyond the pedagogical monopoly the workshop method has exerted on the field of creative writing, as does Dianne Donnelly's *Does the Writing Workshop Still Work?* Katherine Haake's *What Our Speech Disrupts: Feminism and Creative Writing Studies* not only examines the masculinized ways in which creative writing has been imagined, but offers feminist pedagogy through which to reimagine teaching creative writing, while Dianne Donnelly's *Establishing Creative Writing Studies as an Academic Discipline* organizes what emerging scholarship across a range of issues—methodological, pedagogical, and theoretical—in creative writing studies means as the field begins to take prominence in the wider world of English studies. Like Tim Mayers' *(Re)Writing Craft: Composition, Creative Writing, and the Future of English Studies*, I will stake out critical territory in that space and, as a result, address concerns that should be of potential interest to scholars in the field of composition as well as creative writing. The argument this book follows, in other words, is a critical examination of how scholarship between composition and creative writing and how growing discussions about writing in digital environments is developing and will continue to develop within that scholarship.

The historical development of composition studies alongside creative writing, after all, has been, as D. G. Myers and others have illustrated, a double helix of sorts. While both have origins in North American education of the nineteenth century, and while both have set their disciplinary theories and practices on the act of writing, and while both have often (perhaps as a result) found themselves (or at least strands of their scholarship/practices) at odds with the university structure, composition and creative writing have yet to examine together what it means to write across digital environments. Considered at once a space and a set of tools and an ideological matrix, effects of digital environments on the spectrum of writing that at one end we can call "expository" and on the other we can call "creative," stands as yet unconsidered in that history. My hope is that this book will help initiate that discussion.

Creative writing and technology

Since the advent of hypertext, creative writing and new media have produced a spectrum of reactions in scholarship, especially poetry and poetics. While George Landow now canonically explored the ramifications of hypertext on fiction, and Michael Joyce's hypertext short story "Afternoon, A Story" has inspired a whole genre, most work being done at the intersection of creative expression and new media is largely interested in poetics. Loss Pequeno Glazier examines the digital according to three criteria in *Digital Poetics: The Making of E-Poetries*: hypertext, visual/kinetic text, and programmable media. Linking each of these three strands to the work of avant-garde poetry, Glazier argues that the very idea of imaginative writing changes given the materiality of writing across digital media. As a result, "electronic space," Glazier argues, "is the true home of poetry," and electronic environments are inherently "spaces of poesis" (2). Within the span of ten years, scholarly trends linking the poetic to the digital expanded to include C. T. Funkhouser's *Prehistoric Digital Poetry: An Archeology of Forms* and *New Directions in Digital Poetry*; the edited collection *New Media Poetics: Contexts, Technotexts, and Theories*; and *Media Poetry: An International Anthology*. In fact, *Media Poetry* was originally published in 1996 as *New Media Poetry: Poetic Innovation and New Technologies* and republished in 2007 as *Media Poetry: An International Anthology*. The dropping of the word "new" in the title and the inclusion of international works, in the words of Eduardo Kac, "accents the global nature of the movement" and signifies that the development of new media as it intersects with creative expression is no longer a matter of being "new," but rather an essential component one must consider when writing.

In 2014, Lori Emerson extends such thinking, again, along the lines of poetry and poetics, in her book *Reading Writing Interfaces: From the Digital to the Book Bound*, arguing that all inscription technologies—what she calls interfaces—have always mediated writers, texts, and readers and that writers have always been transgressing technological boundaries. Emerson goes so far as to call the interface a "collaborative creative space" and her argument aims to "demystify devices—especially writerly demystification—by opening up how exactly interfaces limit and create certain creative possibilities" (1). While working mostly at the intersection of media archeology and literary studies, Emerson's argument would no doubt have a lot to say to scholars in creative writing studies, especially as that field begins to imagine itself as technologically mediated, or at the very least, interested in the production of imaginative texts across a variety of media.

Perhaps it makes sense that poets and poetry scholars were first to explore what it means to write creatively in a digital age. Poetry is, of course, read through the senses and the kinetic and sensory ways in which new media shape imaginative texts are, obviously, immediately sensual (they are literally seen and heard as much as they are read and interpreted). Language, for the poet, has always been a sensual interface, to use Emerson's word, one that enables ways of being as much as it enables ways of reading. Investigating the symbolic opportunities afforded through emerging communicative interfaces—enabled by digital technologies—seems, in this way, a natural move. Fiction writers, too, however, work not dissimilarly with language and, of course, also write and consider what it means to write across digital technologies; however, we don't often see them represented in the literature on imaginative writing as it has engaged emerging technologies. For this reason, I have chosen to work with examples from fiction and fiction writers as well as poetry and poets in this argument. This is certainly a limit to the argument that I present in the chapters that follow, but one that I hope is corrected by future scholarship that works at the intersection of creative writing and new media.

As the following argument will make clear, the categorical monikers "poet" and "novelist" or "fiction writer" do break down in some ways across digital spaces. That fluidity for some writers, like Ander Monson and David Shields, provides challenges and opportunities not only to examine the tectonic shifts taking place in the culture of contemporary fiction writing, but also to employ conventions from other genres in the formation of new genres. Such symbiotic relationships across genres in digital spaces, in other words, have an effect on how we imagine the subject position we refer to when we refer to "poets" and "novelists." Consider also that digitally born genres, like "Netprov" (the "live" improvisation of storytelling across social media), have appeared in the cultural landscape as well as our scholarship. Emily Short's interactive fiction has asked audiences to reconsider the relationship between imaginative writing and video games, two areas that seem to repel and attract each other equally in the growing space creative writers have made for how the act of imaginative composing intersects with emerging technologies. These developments, I argue in this book, have had an overwhelming effect on how we imagine what it means to write imaginatively across new *and old* technologies.

For example, Rick Moody's tweeted short story "Some Contemporary Characters," while a formally innovative example of digital creative writing, was also, according to him, a way to veer readers away from the screen and back toward the page. (He also said that it felt more like writing haiku, highlighting the ways in which genres tend to interanimate each other in digital environments). Perhaps more than any other field, creative writing remains tied to a print-based industry that makes it a relevant and fascinating space through which to wrestle with the cultural and institutional shifts emerging technologies ask us to consider. The fact that Moody used Twitter as a way to engage with readers who traffic in both electronic and print ecologies speaks volumes regarding where the creative writer stands, culturally and academically, at the start of the twenty-first century. What has become clear is that creative writers and creative writing studies, a disciplinary field that has emerged in its own right at the end of the twentieth century and start of the twenty-first, have already begun to face what it means to write imaginative texts in an age of digital technology. This book works modestly toward contributing to that dialogue by examining the ways in which scholarship in composition studies and creative writing stands to inform what will no doubt become an ongoing dialogue about the role emerging media play in the academic development of the field of creative writing studies.

A note on categorical systems

As the following chapters will show, composition studies and creative writing studies are both academic fields that have historically demonstrated threads of scholarship and practices that put it at odds with the academy. Threads of expressivist research in composition studies, as I will examine in Chapter 1, often seek out the tension between disciplinary conventions and personal voice in order to situate a student writer's literacy and address the power dynamics at work between institution and student writer. Similarly, creative writing studies, as it has begun its own march toward professionalization, as Tim Mayers has argued, often demonstrates what he calls its "institutional conventional wisdom," which claims essentially that the process of creative composition "is something so individual, intrinsic, even mysterious, [that] it cannot really be analyzed or explained in any significant way" (16). Put it in more extreme terms, the Iowa Writers Workshop, the foundational academic creative writing program, which has achieved iconic proportions of influence on creative writing programs across the globe, claims that creative writing cannot be taught. What it means for these fields to be housed in academic departments has been, as a result, a site of debate in both fields. What it hasn't changed is the range of concerns regarding what it means to write, whether in the field of composition or creative writing.

Essentially, our categorical systems and disciplinary differences work to maintain order within our communities. And our communities—to maintain and preserve order—often insist that we adhere to our categories. Working in the shared space between composition and creative writing, this book aims to in some ways reinforce their disciplinary differences (the goal of composition studies will never be, I imagine, the production of professional poets or novelists, just as the goal of creative writing studies will never be to examine and develop literacy practices within and outside of the university) and in some ways to disrupt them (as Wendy Bishop and others have demonstrated, creative writing and composition has each had an impact on the other). Insofar as each of these disciplines is invested in examining writing and its attendant methods of production, they obviously have had and will always have points of contact between them. The argument propelling this book is that the digital humanities has not only emerged as one of those points of contact, but stands to inform their relationship in powerful ways.

Another set of categorical systems any book length argument must consider, especially one interested in emerging technologies, is the definition of terms. There are a number of terms that float through this argument, none of which I invented. All are taken from existing research (e.g., Tim Mayers' "craft criticism") and contextualized as needed, but a few require clarification up front. For example, "multimodal"—the recruitment of different rhetorical modes, visual, aural, textual, in the construction of a text—and "digital" can in some sense be seen as conflated (digital technologies enable multimodality), but require, for my argument, a working consideration of their difference. As Jody Shipka demonstrates in *Toward a Composition Made Whole*, arguments that are quick to conflate digitality and multimodality often fail to address that literacy has always been multimodal (creative or otherwise), even before the advent of digital technologies. One of the contributions I hope the following argument makes is that as creative writing studies begins the work of imagining what it means to approach the act of imaginative composing as a technologically mediated one, it will find a sophisticated home for several kinds of multimodality, like, for example, graphic novels, within its practices and scholarly debates. To examine the digital for the sake of examining the digital is fascinating, in other words, but this is not that book. To learn how to use digital tools is important, but this is not that book. Instead, my interdisciplinary argument aims to explore the impact of technological mediation on creative composition, specifically on how scholars of composition and creative writing imagine authority and subjectivity, genre and process, and pedagogy and institutional practice. Examining those forces within the shared space between composition and creative writing, I will show, points us to powerful ways of imagining both disciplines.

And so I employ a wide ensemble cast in order to stage such a discussion. As mentioned earlier, there are three strands of scholarship at work in my argument—scholarship invested in "creative" or "critical-creative composition" (Macrorie, Sirc, Owens, Rice, Shipka, Wysocki, Johnson), scholarship invested in the intersection of composition studies and creative writing (Bishop, Bloom, Mayers, Ritter, Bizzaro, Vanderslice), and scholarship invested in "creative writing studies" (Harper, Dawson, Donnelly, Haake, Williams)—and my argument recruits and contextualizes those scholars as needed. Indeed, several of those scholars themselves float across borders in their work, but for the sake of clarification I offer the spectrum above. It is within the constellation of those figures that I will trace my argument and it is not the goal of this book to reorganize their contexts or argue for a new configuration of scholarship within writing studies; rather, my goal is to contextualize these voices in regard to each other, using collective terms that work toward making new avenues of knowledge available in both composition and creative writing studies.

I see the digital humanities as a path for creative writing to embrace. An inherently polymorphous development, the digital humanities has emerged halfway through the second decade of the twenty-first century as, to use Charles Bazerman's term, a "disciplined interdisciplinarity." Matthew Kirschenbaum has pointed out that it is "more rooted in English departments than any other departmental home" and as I've already noted elsewhere in this introduction, considerable attention has been paid to it in composition studies, especially in the form of productive explorations of the relationship between writing and technology (Ulmer, Rice, Brooke, Reid). The digital humanities as an intellectual apparatus, of course, is an active part of the academic landscape. The Alliance of Digital Humanities Organizations hosts an annual conference. *Digital Humanities Quarterly* and *Digital Studies* publish work from several disciplines regularly. And edited collections such as the *Blackwell Companion to Digital Humanities*, Matthew Gold's *Debates in the Digital Humanities*, Anne Burdick, Johanna Drucker, Peter Lunenfeld, Todd Presner, and Jeffrey Schnapp's *Digital_Humanities*, and David Berry's *Understanding Digital Humanities* together provide an explosion of scholarship that investigates how various disciplines orient ways of seeing their practices and theories in an age of digital production and consumption. And as Kirschenbaum points out, "digital humanities, which began as a term of consensus among a relatively small group of researchers, is now backed on a growing number of campuses by a level of funding, infrastructure, and administrative commitments that would have been unthinkable even a decade ago" (1).

But what humanist values are at work in the digital humanities relevant to the writer who works across the spectrum of expository and creative writing as they are mediated in digital environments? As Adeline Koh points out, those digital humanities scholars regularly winning grants and funding focus less on "culture than computation [or] projects that focus on digital pedagogy or digital recovery efforts for works by people of color." Koh advocates for a "new wave" of digital humanities, one that has "humanistic questions at its core—because the humanities, centrally, is the study of how people process and document human cultures and ideas, and is fundamentally about asking critical questions of the methods used to document and process. And because these questions can and should be dealt with by people in departments who care about research with undergraduates, by people without the resources to develop the latest and greatest cutting-edge digital humanities tool (which, quite frankly, will be enveloped by commercial industries in the blink of an eye.)" A particularly humanities-inflected understanding of the digital humanities, in other words, stands to powerfully contribute to the ways in which that disciplined interdisciplinarity contributes to the production of knowledge in the academy. Imagined in this way, creative writing's contributions and place alongside composition's work along digital lines stand to bolster the humanist project at stake in imagining humanist research through digital mediations. As the writer becomes increasingly seen as a technologically mediated subject, and as her work becomes increasingly seen as a technologically mediated process and product, composition studies and creative writing studies, as they together examine the ways in which writers and their processes are technologically mediated, are in a powerful place to contribute to the "new wave" of digital humanities research. What better disciplines are there through which to examine the ways cultural production is framed by digital technologies? This book aims to take part in that discussion.

Where I'm going, where I've been

Doug Hesse proposes the metaphor of "fenceless neighbors" to describe the relationship between the fields of composition and creative writing. I find this phrase an apt way of describing how these two fields have interacted since the start of the twenty-first century, a time when composition's digital turn was gaining steam and creative writing began its own formal professionalization. *Kairos* and *Computers and Writing* regularly published articles devoted to investigating the practices and theories attendant to writing across new media. Jeff Rice, Gregory Ulmer, and Byron Hawk advanced arguments for ways of imagining writing in electric and networked environments. And Yancey, Johnson-Eilola, and Samuels (among others) argued that, as Shipka points out, "the disjunction between the multimodal world of communication which is available in the wider community and the conventional print modes of the standard curriculum" is to blame for "students reporting that they feel increasingly alienated from what schools have to offer" (7). Meanwhile, Kenneth Goldsmith's *Uncreative Writing* argued for a kind of poetics that technologically determines the poet as a writer who literally moves words from one context to another. Robert Coover's infamous hypertext fiction course at Brown University, which he wrote about in his ominously titled essay "The End of Books" in Bishop and Ostrom's *Colors of a Different Horse*, was, like hypertext itself, succeeded with scholarship like Trent Hergenrader, Michael Clark, and Joseph Rein's edited collection *Creative Writing in the Digital Age*, in which a variety of authors address in a variety of ways what it means when new and emerging tools and technologies are used for the production of imaginative texts. Despite the rich scholarship in composition investigating the technological mediation of the act of writing and the beginning of a digital turn in creative writing, so far no extended examination of what this means for scholarship between composition and creative writing exists.

I restate this short history here because at the start of the century, while these scholarly advancements took place, I found myself in an English department that allowed me at the time to explore connections between composition and creative writing both in and out of an academic setting. During this time and with considerable help from people from both fields, I cofounded an independent print-based literary magazine (we lasted six years and seven issues before we went on hiatus), which offered me the opportunity to examine the sets of concerns emerging in composition scholarship of the time alongside the demands and practice of creative production. While composition examined how new media and digital technology were reshaping the scene of composition, I found myself a compositionist enmeshed in the wide variety of media it took to publish a literary magazine. My coeditors and I networked (i.e., e-mailed MFA directors, editors, and authors for submissions). We designed a website. We hired a graphic designer. We worked through layout design. We worked with artists who would render visual interpretations for each short story we published. I say this not to point out that technology made all of this possible—writers have, after all, always been technologically mediated—but because while I was learning how to do all of this in a very material way, the field of creative writing studies was in the process of establishing itself as a field with complex methods at the service of producing knowledge about its central object of study: the process of producing imaginative writing.

This book is in many ways the result of the years I spent working on that literary magazine and reading scholarship invested in the intersection of composition and creative writing studies. I point this out in order to say that an argument such as the one I advance in the following chapters works toward understanding the ways in which a theoretically sound and thoroughly examined approach to studying the scene of writing as technologically mediated helps (re)imagine the work that *already* asks the writer to work across a variety of media. The relationship, that is, between the creative writer, her work, and the ways in which her culture situates her and her work, require, not only for the sake of disciplinary knowledge, but larger cultural knowledge as well, a way to work through issues of authority, genre, process, and institutional practice. I suspect that as creative writing studies "further invents" itself as a field, scholars will find a variety of ways through which to sustain such discussions, and this book—through (re)investigating the interdisciplinary state of the relationship between composition studies, creative writing studies, and new media—takes as its premise that creative production, even in a field as print based as creative writing, which has obvious ties and investments in the publishing industry, inevitably dovetails with media of several kinds and it should be the work of the scholar-writer-teacher working in creative writing studies—writing studies in general, really—to scrutinize, study, and survey the peril and possibilities there.

Composition, creative writing studies, and the digital humanities

One of the more striking elements at stake in Hesse's term "creative composition" as he employs it in his essay is that "creative" implies a particular kind of alternative or experimental set of processes for the student writer. "Creative composition" asserts that diverse sets of processes can bring writers to sophisticated understandings of their products as well as nuanced understandings of their process. Many scholars in composition studies would argue that, for the composition student, this is essential work. However, when we examine the work of creative writing studies—an emerging discipline with a growing stake in the quality of the production of imaginative texts—do we see such an alternative or experimental set of processes made available to the writer? The production of a poem or a story or a novel, after all, is often presented in creative writing as a more formal and ultimately conservative process than what composition studies has imagined as "creative." That is to say that the usual assignments in creative writing are often tightly bound up in genre and, therefore, not necessarily "unconventionally" produced. Of course, poetry, fiction, and drama, fully entrenched in specific ways across dozens of textbooks and scholarly articles that perpetuate an often-static definition of the "craft" of writing within those genres, are not "unconventional" at all in the context of creative writing. What does composition studies' scholarship on "creative composing," in other words, have to do with creative writing studies?

Disciplinary relationships and generic conventions are not as rigid or unilateral as the above may suggest. Indeed, as I will later show, the fluidity between them is what generates the question of how such scholarship in composition stands to inform emerging creative writing scholarship and vice versa. By identifying the dialectic above, I merely hope to keep space open throughout my argument that there are areas of creative writing scholarship to which advances in the field of composition studies may not be able to contribute. Just as there are areas of creative writing that do not necessarily inform composition studies. That relationship, as this book will show, is a complex one. But it is that complexity that allows these two areas—each invested in their own ways to the act of writing—to productively inform each other, especially as each has started to inform the other in an age of digital writing.

In Chapter 1, I examine the ways in which creative writing and composition studies have so far examined each in terms of the other—the historical rise of the intersection of composition and creative writing—and the ways in which composition, as a field invested in the study and pedagogy of writing, has imagined itself as a technologically mediated field in order to contextualize our current historical moment: the emergence of the several paths that are made available when we examine the beginning of creative writing's digital turn. More specifically, I examine the role "imagination" has played in composition studies—it has worked as an area in which we store the hope and promise of social, political, and creative ways of imagining the discipline—and how expressivist and neo-expressivist arguments recruiting such an understanding of "imagination" do so in a way that creates tension between the field (and/ or student writer) and the university (as political oppressor), a tension that often puts them at odds with each other, a relationship that we also see echoed in creative writing's status in the university. Turning toward the work of Ken Macrorie, Peter Elbow, Derek Owens, and Geoffrey Sirc, I examine "critical-creative composition," a kind of writing in which aesthetics and imagination are often called upon in order to situate, study, and shape student writing bound up in a particular aesthetic and sociopolitical project. Alongside and after these developments, composition studies moves through a digital turn and creative writing studies establishes itself as an academic discipline. This chapter examines those developments in order to identify a digital trend emerging in creative writing scholarship and point the direction for what further study in this direction entails.

Chapter 2 aims to shape that direction and constructs what I refer to as a "digital branch" of creative writing studies. Drawing from the work of Tim Mayers, who defines what he calls "craft criticism" as discourse and/ or scholarship written by creative writers that address the various forces at work in the production of a creative text (institutional, cultural, political, aesthetic), I extend craft criticism to include the concerns at stake in a digital understanding of creative writing. I turn toward several examples of creative writers, some working within the academy, some not, in order to organize those concerns according to the following categories: author(ity)/subjectivity, genre/process, and institutional practice/areas for further study. The three following chapters take each of those areas up in more detailed examinations.

Specifically, in Chapter 3, I examine how subjectivity and ideology are each technologically mediated within creative writing studies, asking the question: What print-based practices shape the subjectivity framed in the creative writing classroom and how does such framing perpetuate particular ideologies, specifically one that privileges print-based practices and ways of knowing that put it at odds with new and emerging media? What does an ideology that accounts for new media in creative writing look like? Furthermore, what are the implications of creative writing scholars like Kenneth Goldsmith, who have infamously begun the work of framing such an ideology, claiming that appropriation and the "management" of information across digital spaces are not only a new kind of poetics, but also an identity marker (he calls his students and those who subscribe to the practice "thieves" and "plunders")? Are there ethical, political, and cultural elements at stake that, when we examine what it means to be a "creative writer" as a technologically mediated identity, require further exploration and definition? I turn toward the work of Lester Faigley and James Berlin, two scholars highly invested in subjectivity and ideology, respectively, in order to visualize and answer these questions.

Chapter 4 examines the genres and processes produced and employed by the technologically mediated creative writer. Turning toward the work of Walter Ong, Martin Heidegger, and Tim Mayers, I examine Jonathan Franzen's *The Kraus Project*, arguing for a more thorough way of accounting for the ways in which technology has shaped and does shape imaginative expression. Looking at work by artists and writers who write across a variety of media, like Paul Miller, Rick Moody, and Jennifer Egan, I argue for a fluid theory of genre within creative writing studies and more accountability for the variety of processes employed as new genres continue to develop across digital environments. As a result, this chapter points a way toward emphasizing "voice" over genre in creative writing studies, given the polymorphous and quickly evolving nature of genre in digital spaces.

On the one hand, a digital branch of creative writing studies merely sets the stage for scholarship that examines emergent ideologies, processes, and genres of creative expression as they are produced across a variety of media, while on the other, on the programmatic level, it calls for a reorganization of the ways in which creative writing as a discipline imagines itself. Tempering such a call, I present my argument in Chapter 5 as merely the rethinking of the relationship between composition and creative writing, which I argue should both be housed within what Susan Miller (and others) call "writing studies." Such a disciplinary configuration comes with it several benefits, chief among them is the academic valuation of a field where multimodal forms that emerge at an increasing rate (like, for example, the graphic novel) are provided ample space for production and examination. Expanding the interests of creative writing studies to include the digital—and to do so under the aegis of "writing studies" which I demonstrate in this final chapter—requires widening and diversifying the field, programs, courses, and resources for those who teach and practice creative writing in the academy. It is my hope that by calibrating my argument this way, I present a digital branch of creative writing studies as a compliment to composition's digital turn, taking one more step toward the unity of two threads of writing studies uniquely positioned to examine the range of expository and creative processes and products as those processes and products find their place in the digital humanities.

Writers have always, of course, been between worlds. The poet and the Republic. The observer and the participant. Tradition and the individual talent. So we shouldn't be surprised to discover that in academia writing is itself between worlds. Scholarship in composition studies throughout the 1960s, 1970s, and 1980s rose under the gaze of literary studies (Connors, Berlin) just as now, at the dawn of the twenty-first century, the rise of scholarship in creative writing is burgeoning under the gaze of both literary and composition studies (McGurl, Mayers, Myers). Debates on where writing is located, what kind of writing counts, pedagogical methods, and theoretical orientations all undergird the scholarship emerging around composition and creative writing studies. Examining them both in the context of the digital humanities uncovers networks of relations, helping scholar-teachers not only better theorize and understand what we do when we are teaching writing, but, perhaps more importantly, how such practices are always bound up in particular institutional, cultural, political, and aesthetic conditions.

Note

1 There are, of course, exceptions, as this argument will address further on. The work of Dave Starkey, Donald Murray, Wendy Bishop, and Joe Moxley contributed volumes to the relationship between composition, specifically an expressivist inflected understanding of composition, and creative writing. For my purposes here, I mean primarily to point out that the scholarship in composition and rhetoric that worked along a digital turn in that field remained largely unconcerned with neighboring developments in creative writing.

1

Digital Pasts: On Composition, Creative Writing, and Emergent Technologies

Creativity in composition

Even Ann Berthoff tried to warn us: "If the case for composition is made in terms of 'use' in later life, then the chief models [taught] should be the grocery list and the Letter to the Editor" (644). Her essay "From Problem-solving to a Theory of the Imagination," published in the October 1972 issue of *College English*, recounts her layered reaction to the problems she saw in the now infamous Dartmouth Conference of 1966, widely recognized as one of the catalysts for the birth of composition studies. The main effect of that conference, according to her essay, was a stifling of the "creative" and imaginative modes of composing that, she argues, are invaluable parts of the writing process. If composition would come to be defined narrowly by its "uses"—and its genre *par excellence,* the research paper—then it would be reduced to teaching only functional forms through pseudoscientific methods and without the critical capacities to understand writing's value in the socially and culturally constructed worlds (student) writers occupy, a consciousness made possible, she argued, by providing room for writing about and discussing the imaginative work required of the writing process. The institutionalization of composition, historically and symbolically represented by the Dartmouth Conference, Berthoff explains, amounted to a fundamental fissure across the faculties required to learn how to write. Those fissures cracked and formed across what we could now call disciplinary lines:

> The effects of this separation of intellectual and creative modes are not only disastrous pedagogically, but they are also politically suspect. . . . What do we say to the teacher who, as he is personally and professionally dedicated to

helping his disadvantaged students gain the skills which will start them off on an equal footing intellectually, [but now] scorns the "experience theme" because there is no way of getting from this "fun" thing to the "real" thing, i.e., the critical paper? [This teacher] is judging, it seems to me, from a faulty premise: that composition is either self-expression or communication. . . . [And this premise], I would argue, derives from the fundamental misconception which opposes the allegedly creative, personal, emotionally charged, intuitively understood experience to the supposedly intellectual, public, abstract, conceptual non-experience. (646)

The kind of process Berthoff advocates requires the complementary relationship across the above forces and the weaving of those forces into the fabric of any composition course. To compartmentalize the "creative" and exile it from the "critical" and functional work of the composition classroom is, as she puts it, "disastrous" to the teaching of writing. To define that compartmentalization in terms of disciplinary difference, along these lines, is at the very least problematic.

But she had hope. "What is missing," she later explains,

is the understanding of language as an instrument of knowing—our means of knowing our experience, knowing our feelings, knowing our knowledge. . . . We need . . . a philosophy of knowledge which is a theory of imagination [that] could assure us that the choice is not, as the Dartmouth Conference seems to have defined it, between a coruscating discipline and a spiritual and moral freedom. The actual choice, it seems to me, is between a dispiriting regimen, an anti-intellectual manipulation, or a frenetically structured curriculum on the one hand and, on the other, humane instruction claiming as its goal what Coleridge once described as knowing your knowledge. (647)

Much of her scholarship famously worked toward a warning against purely "scientific" ways of framing the writing process in favor of teaching writing as a self-reflexive negotiation of meaning. She worried that composition studies would, put bluntly, ignore or "exterminate" the "chaotic" parts of the writing process, which is where her work located meaningful moments of generative thinking.

I pause on this essay and these selections above to make two observations: we must see disciplinary differences as historically and socially situated within the tradition of English studies (Berthoff did not want to secede imagination and creativity from composition studies as that discipline began to define itself during and after the Dartmouth Conference) and her work "toward a theory of the imagination" in many ways participates in a practice that would by the end of the century frame an explicit call to import aesthetics into composition pedagogy at the same time that field begins to make a digital turn. She describes a beginning for composition's wrestling with the imagination, one that remained largely unconcerned with the emerging field of creative writing for the next two decades, arguably a field that would have much to say about the role of the imagination in the production of a variety of texts, but also a field that largely remained invisible in the academy until the start of the twenty-first century. In other words, what began for compositionists like Berthoff as an investigation into the personal and disciplinary dynamics of process theory (how personal experience and critical acumen both matter [perhaps at different times] to writers learning how "to make meaning"), makes a distinct turn in the late twentieth century by way of empowering such dynamics through incorporating aesthetic ways of knowing and composing into the field of composition studies. Scholars like Derek Owens and Geoffrey Sirc, for example, have each excavated composition's history in order to restore some vital understanding of the role creativity, broadly defined, plays in the study of composition. Their theoretical frameworks for composition would eventually define that field in powerful ways. And they had very little to say about creative writing as a practice or an emerging field.

I am interested in how this line of composition scholarship—one as invested in the critical as it is the creative—has grappled with being "creative." Compositionists within this lineage of scholarship often recruit understandings of "creative" or "imaginative" writing that are synonymous with "unconventional" or "chaotic" or "messy" writing. There is a tendency, generally speaking, to imagine anything "creative" as experimental, shapeless, and/or dangerous. The "imaginative" part of the writing process, along these lines, establishes a way for writers to work their ways toward fundamental understandings of the elements of writing—voice, invention, structure, style—while participating not only in the production of knowledge, but also powerful discoveries of the self and our larger place in the world, which can often look messy and be dangerous. As aesthetics and poetics begin to inform composition studies more explicitly, as this chapter will show, they brought with them not only powerful ways for students to imagine their writing, but also, arguably, liberatory ways for students to understand themselves through their writing. This chapter investigates how such "creativity"—especially as it incorporates the use of aesthetic and poetic forms—reflects the disciplinary evolution of composition studies and how it prepared that field to forge an identity both in cooperation with and resistance to creative writing. Berthoff was not alone in her concerns about the fissures she points to in her 1972 essay, and the work that she and others did in understanding and shaping what I'll call critical-creative composition eventually set the stage for scholars like Wendy Bishop, Patrick Bizzaro, and Tim Mayers to make crucial arguments about what it means to teach writing across the two evolving fields of composition and creative writing later in the twentieth and the start of the twenty-first century. This book examines an emerging digital turn within that borderland scholarship. And this chapter attends to composition and creative writing's historical/disciplinary similarities and differences in order to establish a set of defining criteria regarding what scholarship in the borderland between composition and creative writing entails as it approaches the digital humanities. In the second chapter, I will define and describe that approach so that in the third, fourth, and fifth chapters I can identify how that approach matters for issues regarding (student/writer) subjectivity, genre and process, and future directions for research, respectively.

Invention and imagination in composition

One of the most striking elements of Berthoff's "theory of imagination" is that it attempts to describe what W. Ross Winterowd called the fundamental "mystery" of composition: how writers invent. For Berthoff, invention requires the fundamental assumption that thought and language are interdependent. Writing, along these lines, is not as simple as having a thought and then writing it down. The act of taking thought out of language, for Berthoff, is philosophically impossible and so she examines composing as something bound up in metaphysical relationships that reveal writing as a mode of thinking—one that is necessarily exploratory as well as critical. We discover new meanings when we write and these in turn (re)shape our thinking.

Invention, the creation of new meaning, is therefore a function of a recursive and vigorous process. She calls this "imagination."

Berthoff's scholarship works toward a philosophical impact on the development of what we now call process theory. For her, the imagination is a defining aspect of the active mind, the "shaping power" in which "perception works by forming—finding forms, creating forms, recognizing forms, interpreting forms" (*The Making* 12). We see in her work an attempt not only to protect and value the space of the imagination within the precincts of composition studies, but to define that imagination in specific ways. It is, put simply, a critical apparatus of the writing mind. Informed by a context in which language is empowered to reveal new meanings to the writer, the imagination, for Berthoff, is a critical space reserved for that most critical function of all: invention.

Stephen North, in *The Making of Knowledge in Composition: Portrait of an Emerging Field*, describes Berthoff's contributions to composition as "highly influential" and claims that—beyond the construction of her philosophy for teaching writing—the central force in her work points the field toward the necessity to examine our practices in light of sound and sustainable theories. That the field of composition studies was in the process of staking out a variety of methods regarding the study of writing during the time of Berthoff's writing—almost problematically so (he describes it as a "methodological land rush")—means that in order to situate that contribution, we must sift through a variety of terms that sometimes mean slightly different things in different contexts. For example, terms like "process" and "imagination" for Berthoff mean something else to expressivists, who, working around the same time as Berthoff, found in those terms openings that they used to invite innovative forms into the teaching of composition also under the aegis of "imagination."

Expressivist arguments of the 1960s and 1970s often contextualized students and the study of composition as an act always framed by dominant sociopolitical practices. They also addressed the implications of process, citing imagination and creativity as important resources for the writer, but with one important difference: imagination came with the promise of combating oppressive power dynamics in the composition classroom. Expressive discourse—understood broadly as the process of constructing a text through addressing emergent relationships between writer and text, language and expression, and the dynamic ways in which those relationships open up crucial understandings of that writer's literacy and place in the world—defines a process that often recruits the use of "creative" forms, like collage, memoir, and freewriting. Imagination, in other words, wasn't just a natural part of the writing process (that could be used in the service of strengthening and innovating student literacy), but also a vital path toward a more complex understanding of our humanity in political and cultural terms. In fact, one of the reasons for the Dartmouth Conference in the first place was to examine the practices of writing instruction, which were later seen by expressivists to be largely product driven and what Lad Tobin called "correction-obsessed." A growing unease began to take form around "traditional" writing instruction and expressivist scholarship of this time began to emphasize "innovative" approaches to using and teaching writing. Again, in the words of Lad Tobin, these scholars "were speaking up for students, freedom, innovation, creativity, and change" (5).[1]

This notion that "creativity" is a valuable part of a sociopolitical project aimed at serving student literacy through a transformative pedagogy that works toward the ethical (re)production of citizens capable of using their literacy to work their way out of oppressive power structures is, to put it simply, ambitious. For our purposes here, it is enough to notice that "creativity" is used as a vehicle for what some people might call transformative pedagogy. The way to transformation, along the lines of these arguments, is through importing into composition studies marginalized discourses that speak from outside the dominant structures of the university—to recruit "creative" writing assignments. To imagine marginalized discourses as *creative* or as remedies to the "correction-obsessed" and oppressive literacy structures of the university requires, as Berthoff would also point out, that we examine such practices in light of sound and sustainable theories. In what follows, I'll sketch critical-creative composition as a way of framing how creativity works within that field so as to situate the larger discussion(s) that take place across the fields of composition and creative writing later in the twentieth century, which I will examine toward the end of this chapter. As composition carves out critical space for creativity and makes a digital turn in the process, creative writing begins to emerge as an academic discipline. What follows works toward understanding how that digital turn affects the growing body of scholarship that, by the start of the twenty-first century, becomes explicitly interested in, as Wendy Bishop puts it, crossing the borders between composition and creative writing.

Critical-creative composition

In 1973, Peter Elbow wrote his way around the power dynamics of the student-teacher dichotomy in *Writing Without Teachers,* famously constructing a student-centered writing program that worked toward identifying ways for writers to develop understandings of voice, style, and form that worked largely through the construction of the self-sponsored writing tasks those writers decided were important enough to write about. His project did a lot of work for compositionists who sought to empower student writing in a way that did not perpetuate what they saw as oppressive university structures of disciplinarity. By 1985 Ken Macrorie, in *Telling Writing,* resituates such counter-institutional space within the institution, arguing for a less "dry" kind of writing to be produced in composition courses, a kind of writing that avoided what he called "Engfish," a discourse within which student expression has become so deformed by institutional structures of disciplinarity as to no longer mean anything. Macrorie is interested in teaching a kind of writing with "no phoniness, no pretension" (64). For him, "most good writing is clear, vigorous, honest, alive, sensuous, appropriate, unsentimental, rhythmic, without pretension, fresh, metaphorical, evocative in sound, economical, authoritative, surprising, memorable, and light" and to cultivate such writing is to open the process of composition up to include innovative forms that, for him, encourage such qualities, as opposed to the tired forms of traditional academic discourse (65). To compose, along the lines established by Elbow and Macrorie's arguments, is to invite "chaos" (Elbow's term) into the writing process, to take advantage of the benefits offered through "creative" forms and critical approaches to/through those forms, which will, so the arguments go, strengthen and empower student writing through the vigor promised by creativity as well as the possibility of political and cultural transformation, both for the student who participates in it and the university structure that provides space for it.

What's important to point out here is that, as composition studies continues carving out disciplinary space for itself, it does so while also maintaining a thread of discourse invested in writing outside of institutional and disciplinary structures. In *Writing Without Teachers*, Elbow imagines this literally, defining a process of writing (linked to his working metaphor of writing as cooking) uninvolved with the power dynamics of the university system in general or the composition classroom (as it could have been defined by the Dartmouth Conference) specifically. Elbow's argument, therefore, has a twofold impact: it is about writing outside of disciplinarity and yet it is a book widely read by professionals within the discipline of composition studies. Uniting this twofold impact is the fact that his book is about textual generation and the "freedom" to invite creativity (as opposed to static disciplinary forms) into the scene of writing. Writers, in Elbow's argument, commit themselves to creativity as it can be understood to be an oscillation between "chaos and disorientation" and "control, growth, and development." Macrorie works within such double-effect as well, simultaneously making space for a kind of writing that is counter-institutional, but, in his case, produced within the institution. He wants students to avoid "Engfish" through, what he names in his book *Uptaught*, "a third way": a path toward mutual respect on behalf of faculty and students working through instructive dialogue in order to help students produce texts that are "worthwhile," which doesn't necessarily require them to emerge within disciplinary forms.

By 1993 Derek Owens, in *Resistant Writings (and the Boundaries of Composition)*, extends Macrorie's line of thinking, arguing that the "resistant" space between student and institution can be a fertile soil:

> Many ideas simply cannot make themselves heard within the conventions of the tradition; for many, resisting forms are the only way for certain thoughts to evolve and take shape. Ideas, after all, never exist "outside" of forms, but are themselves forms. Perhaps worse, if we assume that any and all important ideas must surface within standard English and academic discourse, we display a depressing lack of imagination. If anything, it's this sense of the imaginative I want to foreground in the writing classroom. I want writing to be exciting, risky, strange; dull, safe, conventional texts put me and my students to sleep. I suppose I see my job as keeping myself from automatically succumbing to the hypnotic rhythms of the obligatory,

the required, and the institutionally sanctioned talk of the academy. If, after tasting an array of oppositional forms—those "resisting" writings—they choose to remain in the conventional (as have I, on many occasions), fine. But at least the decision will be theirs, not mine. (17)

The writing process, as established through this line of composition scholarship, requires space for an imagination that frees the student through a discourse that privileges her authority, experience, and creativity. To resist a "depressing lack of imagination" is to commit to what Elbow calls "chaos and disorientation" and the dialectic of the discovery and construction of meaning invited into the scene of composition when, as Owens puts it, such imagination is foregrounded. The forms such scholarship tend to advocate in order to construct this scene of composition recur throughout their arguments: freewriting, autobiographical writing, collage/montage, narrative, poetry, pastiche, playful texts, and fragmented texts appear across these arguments as forms that are in themselves creative and imaginative as well as vehicles for inviting student writing that is creative and imaginative. For Elbow, these forms (freewriting, autobiography/journal writing, and fragments especially) are at the service of learning how to become a stronger writer, that is, one who writes with clarity and purpose. For Macrorie and Owens they are at the service of learning how to invigorate one's prose not only for the sake of strengthening one's writing, but also for strengthening one's understanding of her role in the cultural and socially constructed world she occupies.

Almost a decade after Owens' *Resisting Writings*, Geoffrey Sirc's *English Composition as a Happening* situates such forms in an excavation of the avant-garde tradition that, he argues, has been "a path not taken" within composition studies. By (re)framing our compositional space to include "the radical gestures of the Happenings artists," Sirc argues for a space that is itself innovative:

We became moderns. But I couldn't stop thinking about, for example, Ken Macrorie, and this book of his, *Uptaught*, which read like Kurt Vonnegut's long-lost foray into Composition Theory. How did we go from a book like Macrorie's, urging "that teachers must find ways of getting students to produce (in words, pictures, sounds, diagrams, objects or landscapes) what students and teachers honestly admire," to meditating on "Texts as Knowledge Claims: The Social Construction of Two Biologists' Articles?" Suddenly, spirit, love, adventure, poetry, incense, kicky language, and rock 'n roll were gone. The forms and constraints seemed overwhelming, the huge gray University walls had grown tall and imposing, keeping the revelers out. As I read further through this new epistemic, Modernist Composition, I noticed something else—call it Composition's material restraint, the phenomenon by which a *de facto* "Composition Canon" forms, with the same names cropping up not just in an anthology tables of contents, but in "Works Cited" lists. As article after article appeared, one could trace the waxing and waning of theoretical trends: Langer, Polanyi, Vygotsky, Odell, Emig, Berthoff, Bruffee, Bartholomae, Berlin, Anzaldua, Foucault, and Freire. This narrow-banding is curious for a discipline that trumpets the value of linguistic richness. (7–8)

Both Sirc and Owens make explicit calls to (re)include "imagination" and "poetry" within the realm of composition—an impulse that has been within composition studies in some fashion at least ever since the Dartmouth Conference (and the scholarship that followed in its wake) helped establish the field as we know it today. In lining up composition's history with art history, Sirc goes so far as to find new techniques, which, for him,

include, besides the standard freewriting, listing, drafting, etc., appropriating, sampling, copying, cataloging, scanning, indexing, chatting, and audio/video-streaming (think of these as a new list of gerunds to supersede Bartholomae's knowing, selecting, evaluating, reporting, concluding, and arguing). If a Happening or Duchamp's Large Glass or a Rauschenberg combine-painting or a Beuys multiple or a Koons sculpture are typical examples of avant-garde art, we might think of synchronous/asynchronous conversation transcripts, Story-Space hypertexts, Web pages, emails, or even informal drafts as species of avant-garde composition. (19)

These calls to examine what it means to include the teaching of imaginative forms—critical-creative composing—have two major repercussions that I would like to examine.

First of all, critical-creative composition seems to be very concerned with imagination as a dialectic between form and formlessness, disciplinarity and nondisciplinarity. On the one hand, creativity is a matter of form: poetry, narrative, collage, etc. In a field where developing student literacy—argumentative writing, clear thinking, critical intervention—is at the heart of the endeavor, including imaginative forms like poetry can seem problematic.

How are students supposed to learn about writing a sound argument by writing a poem? But when the focus of the field shifts to include the process of constructing a text, as process theory and expressivism shifted the field of composition through the 1970s and 1980s, such inclusions, of course, make more sense. Students can use poetry, for example, as a way of addressing structure and style, among other things, in the active construction of texts that contribute to critical discussions on what it means to write within their particular institutional, cultural, and political circumstances. Their creativity can serve their critical literacy. (Or resist it). They can also, as Owens suggests, make other ideas heard, ideas that cannot be expressed "within the convention of the tradition." There is a striking belief in form as a way toward widening the expressive scope of a composition course—to help students see that meaning is always rhetorically situated and that different forms will have different effects in different contexts—and that such literacy opens up the possibility for composition to do sociopolitical work. Form, this line of thinking suggests, is one way toward Berthoff's desire to retain the imagination in the composition classroom. However, the functions of these forms (as opposed to the hyperfunctional grocery list and Letter to the Editor that Berthoff points out earlier) as well as their functionlessness provides the dialectic within which critical-creative composition emerges. In other words, in order to help students through the production of a variety of forms, these arguments tend to point toward the "messiness" of the exploratory (and sometimes formless) process of generating, discovering, and critically shaping what eventually becomes form or text. I point these out here not to dispute them, but to describe them. I see this as a striking claim for the field of composition studies to make regarding how creativity factors into its theoretical and pedagogical imperatives. I will address the contrast between such an understanding of creative work and the field of creative writing's largely different understanding of creative work (which is surprisingly more conservative) later in this chapter, then reconcile the two within their technological mediation made possible by examining them in light of the digital humanities.

Berthoff's understanding of imagination worked toward an understanding of form as the process through which students came to recognize/construct meaning within/across its construction in particular knowledge communities. Her project, while coinciding with the expressivist movement, and in some ways overlapping with it (they both invest in the power of exploratory methods within composition and see such exploration as paths toward invention), bares an important difference insofar as she considers epistemic and disciplinary ways of knowing to be intimately bound up in the ways through which student writers explore, negotiate, and create through form. In other words, Berthoff's "theory of the imagination" anticipates much of the rhetorical scholarship of the 1980s and 1990s that examined and advocated for epistemic theories of composition. As James Berlin puts in it *Rhetoric and Reality*, in this view, the writer, language, and reality are determined by "what can be known, how it can be known, and how it can be communicated" (766). So while Berthoff called for imagination as a vital component of the composing process, she did so in a way that called for disciplinarity and the production of (institutional) knowledge.

Expressivist arguments (like Macrorie and Elbow) and neo-expressivist arguments (like Owens and Sirc) tend to recruit imagination in arguments that work toward the nondisciplinary (re)production of what Macrorie called "worthwhile" writing, not necessarily the reproduction of disciplinary discourse. This tension—between form and formlessness, disciplinarity and nondisciplinarity—marks a productive contrary within composition studies and how it imagines "creativity." I will address the counterpart of this tension—disciplinary and nondisciplinary line crossing—in terms of creative writing studies toward the end of this chapter.

Secondly, composition's imagination is highly invested in transformation. Seen as a sociopolitical project through which writers practice and examine creative forms that can shed some light on the way they imagine textuality and the discursive worlds they occupy (and their attendant politics), imagination for someone like Owens or Sirc brings composition studies closer to the sublime, a space where students encounter their own literacy in a way that revolutionizes their understanding of self, text, and world, or, at the very least, the tensions between that triangulation. Such transformation as it concerns creative writing studies will be the subject of Chapter 3.

I bring up these two prongs of critical-creative composition (form/disciplinarity and transformation) here because I see this current running through arguments that make a digital turn in composition scholarship as well as arguments advocating for the emerging discipline of creative writing studies, two swarms of scholarship that began to appear toward the end of the twentieth and beginning of the twenty-first century. As creative writing continues its process of (re)imagining itself within the academy and as composition (re)defines theory/practice around digital environments, a new relationship between those two fields—composition and creative writing—becomes possible.

Composition, new media, and the rise of creative writing studies

New media's influence on the scene and discipline of composition studies has been, of course, widely recognized. In her 1998 chair's address at the Conference on College Composition and Communication, Cynthia Selfe directs the field's attention to the need to "think about what we are doing and [to understand] at least some of the important implications of our actions" when we admit to the fact that "technology is inextricably linked to literacy and literacy education in this country." Urging that compositionists not satisfy themselves with merely using computers as a "tool" in the classroom, Selfe's address evokes a moral obligation to attending to the ways technology and literacy are inextricably bound to each other—and that a refusal to think through their relationship contributes to the perpetuation of unfair educational systems that "enact social violence and ensure continuing illiteracy under the aegis of education" (1166). She goes on to explain:

> We need to recognize that we can no longer simply educate students to become technology users—and consumers—without also helping them learn how to become critical thinkers about technology and the social issues surrounding its use. When English/language arts faculty require students to use computers in completing a range of assignments—without also providing them the time and opportunity to explore the complex issues that surround technology and technology use in substantive ways—we may, without realizing it, be contributing to the education of citizens who are habituated to technology use but who have little critical awareness about, or understanding of, the complex relationships between humans, machines, and the cultural contexts within which the two interact. Composition teachers, language arts teachers, and other literacy specialists need to recognize that

the relevance of technology in the English studies disciplines is not simply a matter of helping students work effectively with communication software and hardware, but, rather, also a matter of helping them to understand and to be able to assess—to pay attention to—the social, economic, and pedagogical implications of new communication technologies and technological initiatives that affect their lives. Knowledgeable literacy specialists at all levels need to develop age-appropriate and level-appropriate reading and writing activities aimed at this goal. This approach—which recognizes the complex links that now exist between literacy and technology at the end of the twentieth century—constitutes a critical technological literacy that will serve students well. (1181)

Selfe advocates for a critical literacy that new technological environments situate around contemporary literacy—and asks all strands of English studies to explore what such a critical literacy entails. I pause on Selfe's comments above not only because they serve as an important origin point for composition studies and its digital turn, but because she alerts the field to the critical, structural, and even ethical imperatives at work in such a turn. Furthermore, how does creative writing—a vital and growing part of the disciplines Selfe identifies above—see itself within such a paradigm?

Those compositionists who took up Selfe's call to action (Rice, Wysocki, Sirc) saw the development of what it means to imagine writing as a networked set of practices that continually position writers between the texts that they make and what it means to write such texts. A wealth of scholarship on teaching and developing ways of imagining writing that included a range of creative-critical forms—hypertext, blogs, visual and aural rhetoric, as well as the forms Sirc advocates in *English Composition as a Happening*, "freewriting, listing, drafting, appropriating, sampling, copying, cataloging, scanning, indexing, chatting, and audio/video-streaming . . . synchronous/asynchronous conversation transcripts, Story-Space hypertexts, Web pages, emails, or even informal drafts"—began to emerge in pedagogically and theoretically framed articles across journals like *Computers and Composition* and the online *Kairos: A Journal of Rhetoric, Technology, Pedagogy*. Digital spaces, it seems, make perfect sense for compositionists interested in critical-creative composition.

In *The Rhetoric of Cool: Composition Studies and New Media*, Jeff Rice addresses these changes by reaching further back than the Dartmouth Conference, isolating the year 1963 as that transformative moment when composition confronts issues regarding technology. Rice identifies that such a technological reframing of writing not only upsets the conventions of composition-as-usual, but also opens up new points of departure for the field, points made available by moving beyond the field's impulse to define itself in narrow and restricting ways:

> The very act of restriction controls the field's perception of itself and ability to re-present itself in a variety of ways, especially if those ways conflict or disrupt our expectations. The restriction keeps one imaginary element in place (what we imagine ourselves to be doing or what we imagine ourselves to be) and shuts out another (what we imagine we might become). No truer has this claim I make been than with the role of technology in writing instruction. (19)

Rice positions composition as a field that promotes understandings of and interventions within a range of compositional options made available through electronic writing, acknowledging a series of new practices that emerge when we do so. The chapters of his book break these practices down and (re)turn us to histories of composition in the process, identifying chora, appropriation, juxtaposition, commutation, nonlinearity, and imagery as those compositional features attendant to electronic writing practices.

The act of restriction that he addresses in the above quote might as well apply to creative writing as it began to emerge as a field at least marginally interested in writing instruction in the academy at the end of the twentieth century. In fact, the same year Selfe gave her chair's address at the Conference on College Composition and Communication (CCCC), Wendy Bishop published *Elements of Alternate Style,* an edited collection featuring essays by some of the most well-regarded scholars in composition and creative writing at the time, assembling ways of approaching the writing classroom through hybridized discourses/assignments that used "alternative" and/or "creative" approaches to writing alongside traditional ones. Bishop's work, along with Katherine Haake, Patrick Bizzaro, Dave Starkey, Lynn Bloom, Kelly Ritter, and Stephanie Vanderslice, began the work of imagining new relationships across composition and creative writing. I'm not so interested right now in the fact that those connections went largely without attempts to locate the role technology can/should play in creative writing. Rather, I'm interested in pointing out that composition's evolution into a field highly invested in critical-creative composing—those alternative and creative assignments/ approaches toward teaching writing—led it naturally to creative writing. And it attracted those scholars in creative writing who were also concerned with the status of their work in the academy.

While compositionists were forming ways of framing critical-creative approaches toward composition, scholars in the field of creative writing were forming ways of engaging with compositionists, largely according to the two criteria we see compositionists appealing to in their arguments for creative approaches to teaching writing: form/disciplinarity and transformation. Wendy Bishop's *Elements of Alternate Style* and Lynn Bloom's *Composition Studies as a Creative Art*, for example, stand as formative examples. Both fuse the fields of composition and creative writing. In the case of *Elements of Alternate Style*, that fusion is at the service of the tensions between traditional academic forms and creative ones. As Patricia Suzanne Sullivan points out,

> There are essays on how to experiment with crots (a kind of paragraph fragment), lists, labyrinthine sentences, sentence fragments, collage, montage, repetition with words and phrases, double-voiced styles (in the form of writing in columns or juxtaposed as paragraphs), paragraphs of only one syllable words, fractured narratives, and alternative or creative research projects, as well as other writing assignments and exercises that emphasize wordplay, improvisation, rhythm, playing with perspective and point of view shifts, electronic chats, and so on. (25)

Whereas, in the case of *Composition Studies as a Creative Art*, that fusion is at the service of the transformative: "the essence," Bloom claims, "of regarding composition studies as a creative art is to engage in a process of intellectual or aesthetic free play, and to translate the results of this play into serious work that retains the freedom and play of its origins . . . *we live the questions while we seek the answers*" (4, emphasis mine). For Bishop, there is a striking familiarity in the two fields of composition and creative writing, one that shows us the value of teaching critical-creative forms often considered to be outside the "tradition"—just as Owens and Sirc claim—while for Bloom there is a striking familiarity in the field of composition and creative writing insofar as both of those fields are invested (or can be further invested) in ways of understanding writing as a way toward personal reinvention—just like Elbow and Macrorie point out. In other words, while research in composition studies moved toward critical, and in some cases paradigm shifting, understandings of the relationship between technology and literacy, creative writing reached out to its counterparts in composition studies. The traffic between these two fields largely moved along two avenues: form and transformation.

By the end of the twentieth century, composition and creative writing were two fields within English studies ready for continued discussion regarding what it means to teach writing and the role that form/disciplinarity and transformation play in those processes. By the start of the twenty-first century, composition's formation into a discipline invested in critical-creative approaches toward the teaching of writing made it a natural ally for scholars who were also interested in creative writing. The work of Dave Starkey and his edited collection *Teaching Writing Creatively* (published the same year as Selfe's CCCC chair's address) addresses the range of concerns that emerge when we consider breaking down the definitions of "creative" and "academic" writing. Katherine Haake's *What Our Speech Disrupts* (2000) examines the perpetuation of problematically musicalized notions and definitions of "creativity" and "writer" that go on when we refuse to theorize within the field of creative writing. Patrick Bizzaro's *College English* article "Research and Reflection in English Studies: The Special Case of Creative Writing" (2004) works toward framing the kind of research and knowledge production that can take place in a more highly theorized field of creative writing. Kelly Ritter and Stephanie Vanderslice's *Can It Really Be Taught? Resisting Lore in Creative Writing Pedagogy* examines the pedagogical imperative of the emerging field. Then came Bishop and Starkey's *Keywords in Creative Writing* (2006), D. G. Myers historical account of creative writing, *The Elephants Teach: Creative Writing Since 1885* (2006), Tim Mayers's *(Re)Writing Craft: Composition, Creative Writing, and the Future of English Studies (2007)*, and Mark McGurl's *The Program Era*, which reads postwar American fiction through the lens of the field that McGurl argues is most influential in its production: the field of creative writing.[2]

What does any of this have to do with the digital turn in composition studies? By the end of the twentieth century and the start of the twenty-first, composition and creative writing were two fields within English studies already beginning continued discussion regarding what it means to teach writing and the role that form/disciplinarity and transformation plays in those processes. Each field did so both independently and in relation to each other: composition's formation into a discipline invested in critical-creative approaches toward the teaching of writing, of course, firmly establishes that the field's digital turn would not only be a reimagining of the field in many ways, but also an acknowledgment that the field is capable of distinct discussions with other disciplines regarding what it means to write. It just so happens that creative writing was firmly establishing itself as one of those disciplines. The natural question, the major one that this book aims to answer, is: What do those interdisciplinary conversations look like as creative writing begins to enter the discussions composition makes possible in digital environments?

Creative writing and the digital humanities

One of the major pieces of scholarship within that borderland is Tim Mayers's *(Re)Writing Craft: Composition, Creative Writing, and the Future of English Studies*. In that book, Mayers situates that emerging scholarship within an alliance between the fields of composition and creative writing, amplifying a call to further fuse the two fields by isolating what he calls the "institutional conventional wisdom" of creative writing in the academy: "Briefly summarized, this institutional-conventional wisdom holds that creativity or writing ability is fundamentally 'interior' or 'psychological' in nature and that it is thus the province only of special or gifted individuals and is fundamentally unteachable" (14). Such wisdom obviously puts creative writing in a strange place in the academy. The forms the field teaches—poetry, fiction, sometimes drama and creative nonfiction—don't require the criticism-as-usual ordinarily associated with English departments, and as a result, as Mayers points out, even creative writers within the academy view criticism or theory suspiciously. As his argument unfolds, he makes a striking case for how this holds back creative writers, citing several of the scholars I review here in his overall claim that the field of creative writing already, whether it admits it or not, consents to theoretical positions regarding the teaching of imaginative writing (to say that it is unteachable is itself a theoretical position) and that, furthermore, the embracing, examination, and/or widening of those positions stand not only to invigorate creative writing programs, but its very place as a subspecialty within English studies at large.

In order to do so, he calls on Martin Heidegger's phenomenological investigation of human consciousness—and its relation to poetry, language, and thought:

> Specifically, what Heidegger does is to look to "correct" (the everyday, commonsense, dominant conceptions about things) in order to find pathways to the "true" (the ontologically "primordial" essences of things). . . . For Heidegger, the everyday, commonsense notions about things, while correct, tend to conceal far more than they reveal. And in many cases, what gets concealed is far more important, and far more essential, that what gets revealed. (69)

Poetry, for Heidegger, is, of course, one major way through which Being reveals itself. For Mayers, Heidegger's understanding of craft "eradicates the problematic and artificial distinction between craft and talent"—essentially through emphasizing that poetry is produced not through an innate talent, but rather through the complex manipulation of not only tools like meter and rhyme, but also the poet's relationship with language, all of which are at everybody's disposal all the time—we simply conceal that when we claim invention is the result of innate talent. For Mayers, Heidegger is important for several reasons. His theory sheds light on how poetry is written and what it means to write poetry, not to mention what using his theory to understand the creative process means for a discipline that is still understanding its role in the academy. (It widens and deepens the theoretical positions creative writers can make regarding what it is they do and how they do it). Most importantly, though, Heidegger serves as a resource for craft critics who, according to Mayers's argument, participate in an ongoing dialogue about the conditions surrounding creative production. Craft, for Mayers, is more than the surface features of a text (or the "tools" one employs in order to produce a text). It is, rather, a complex network of social, cultural, and institutional forces that contribute to the production of an imaginative text. Craft criticism is the professional discourse creative writers employ when addressing those wider concerns situated around the production of a text.

Mayers also points us toward Heidegger's understanding of poetry as it relates to technology. While for Mayers this relationship is important primarily in contextualizing Heidegger's contribution to Mayers's definition of craft criticism, I find it a valuable starting point for how composition and creative writing's ongoing discussions regarding writing take shape within the digital humanities. As Mayers puts it:

> To this essence of technology, this mode of revealing, Heidegger applies the name "enframing." Enframing sets things "in order," so to speak, so that "everywhere everything is ordered to stand by, to be immediately at hand," indeed to stand there just so that it may be called for further ordering. Whatever is ordered about in this way has its own standing. We call it the "standing-reserve." As an example of this concept, Heidegger considers a hydro-electric plant on the Rhine River. In response to the demand for electricity along the network of cables supplied by this power plant, the river itself becomes standing-reserve. It is ordered to stand on call, to become a supplier of electric power that is dispensed on demand. In response to the anticipated objection that the river nevertheless "is still a river in the landscape," Heidegger writes: "Perhaps. But how? In no other way than as an object on call for inspection by a tour group ordered to go there by the vacation industry." The ultimate danger in this, according to Heidegger, is that eventually human beings will come to conceive of everything, including themselves, *only* as standing-reserve. (70, original emphasis)

We can hear Selfe's call to consider the relationship between literacy and technology refract through the way I have framed Mayers and Heidegger here. The revealing that Mayers uses Heidegger to illustrate urges us not to conceal the critical relationships (and the conditions of creative production) at stake when we examine writing in light of digital technologies. After all, for Heidegger technology was one of the great concealers: it created standing-reserves all around us. Selfe asks us to consider technology itself and how it frames literacy. She set in motion a line of thinking that worked toward revealing what it means to write in/with technology. What would it mean for us to examine the technological conditions of the production of imaginative writing in light of the digital turn provided by such pioneering work in composition studies?

While that is the larger question of this book, I want to settle a foundation on which we can construct those answers through linking the currents I have identified so far in this chapter. Berthoff's work toward a "theory of the imagination," one that is bound up in a project aimed at helping students "know their knowledge," is in many ways answered by Mayers' craft criticism, a kind of knowledge that examines the institutional, cultural, and social conditions surrounding the production of imaginative texts. That we can make such a connection is the product of two fields coming together in innovative ways over the course of at least a decade. Furthermore, Selfe's framework for understanding the relationship between literacy and technology underscores the ways in which any investigation regarding the relationship between creative writing and (its role within) the digital humanities should certainly entail emphasizing the humanities—and the questions that the humanities are uniquely suited to answer—as it seeks to move the field forward in such discussions. In other words, I do not aim with this book to merely outline tools—what Heidegger would call "standing-reserves"—but rather the sustained examination of those tools and the social, cultural, and institutional forces that surround them. In this way, I want to work alongside Jeff Rice's claim that "the very act of restriction controls the field's perception of itself and ability to re-present itself in a variety of ways, especially if those ways conflict or disrupt our expectations" (19). If creative writing stands to (re) invent itself as it moves forward into deeper considerations of its technological environments, then, as Rice points out, such movement may necessarily require an opening up of that field along the lines of form and transformation that have always, as I hope this chapter has demonstrated, worked between the fields of composition and creative writing.

Notes

1   Quoted from Patricia Suzanne Sullivan's *Experimental Writing in Composition: Aesthetics and Pedagogies*.

2   While McGurl's argument is a powerful one—he reads postwar American fiction alongside the historic rise of creative writing programs, arguing that creative writing programs have had the strongest effect on postwar American literature, a largely homogenizing effect—he does not represent the research that I am presenting here.

2

Defining Digital Creative Writing Studies

In January 2009, *College English* devoted a special issue to the status of creative writing in the twenty-first century. In the introduction to that special issue, guest editors Kelly Ritter and Stephanie Vanderslice address the crossroads at which creative writing finds itself through

> pos[ing] the following central questions: What is Creative Writing as it enters the twenty first century? What new facets of this discipline are emerging? What new questions need to be raised in order to keep the discipline engaged, productive, and respected well into this new millennium? (214)

The issue expands on the problems and possibilities that creative writing faces in the twenty-first century through essays that grapple with a wide range of concerns. Mary Ann Cain's "To Be Lived: Theorizing Influence in Creative Writing" examines and advocates for creative writing's resistance to institutional hegemonic forces. Patrick Bizzaro's "Writers Wanted: Reconsidering Wendy Bishop" urges the merging of expressivism and social epistemic rhetoric. And Tim Mayers's "One Simple Word: From Creative Writing to Creative Writing Studies" calls on scholars and teachers of creative writing to recognize an emerging field of creative writing studies in order to better theorize and understand the effects of creative writing's academic institutionalization on the imaginative texts produced there. Since that issue, several of these concerns have been explored through edited collections like Dianne Donnelly's *Does the Writing Workshop Still Work?*—which examines the workshop method through not just pedagogical, but institutional, historical, and ontological concerns—and in book length arguments like Paul Dawson's *Creative Writing and the New Humanities*, in which he examines "what form a literary intellectual might take in the age of postmodernity . . . and what role Creative Writing can play in the formation of literary intellectuals" (5).

And while all this work admirably approaches some of the urgent pedagogical, methodological, and institutional concerns developing in creative writing, one set of concerns remains largely unaddressed: the ways in which creative writing, or creative writing studies, engages with, understands, responds to, and thrives in an age of digital writing.

In this chapter, I define and examine a digital branch of creative writing studies. Defining creative writing studies in the words of Katharine Haake as "scholarly work that 'seeks to move us beyond our preoccupation with the writer or the text to the role of creative writing as an academic discipline inside a profession that includes, but is not limited to, the production and teaching of imaginative writing'" (quoted in "One Simple Word" 218), Tim Mayers urges scholars to explore the "problems and internal contradictions" that present themselves through the introduction of the word "studies" to "creative writing" so as to form a complex theoretical and pedagogical discourse regarding the rich opportunities available when we deepen and explore the various ways creative writing has been imagined. And in the twenty-first century, obviously, poetry, short stories, and creative nonfiction live—are written and read—across our digital technologies. But in what ways have their digital environments begun to affect them? What can creative writing studies help us understand about those effects? And most importantly, how does writing "creatively" in digital spaces alter the act of composing "creatively" and help teachers, writers, and scholars of creative writing (and composition studies) better theorize our current methods and practices? By working toward an answer to the latter question, this chapter establishes a framework to examine what emerges when, following Mayers's lead, we add "one simple word": *digital* creative writing studies.

Creative writing scholarship and "craft criticism"

As many scholars working at the intersection of composition studies and new media have argued, the methodological complexity that emerges when examining the act of composing with new media provides scholars the chance to reevaluate fundamental assumptions attendant to established methods. And in an era of blurred generic boundaries, multimedia storytelling, and open source culture, creative writing scholars stand poised to consider the role technology—and the creative writer's playful engagement with technology—have occupied in the evolution of its practices. To get there from here, however, I will begin by contextualizing and addressing the ways Tim Mayers's argument for creative writing studies comes from a history of creative writing scholarship that he recruits and redirects toward a practice he calls "craft criticism." I will then extend craft criticism through some of what composition studies, literary studies, and new media studies have explored regarding the ways digital environments help us reimagine imaginative texts and the composing process. I hope to come out on the other end with a way of imagining what it means to work with a digital craft criticism and, ultimately, in the chapters that follow, what digital craft criticism means for creative writing studies and English studies at large.

I use Mayers's pioneering book *(Re)Writing Craft: Composition, Creative Writing, and the Future of English Studies* as a touchstone for research on creative writing not only because of the useful understanding of the institutional context he builds around that field but also because of the larger context he builds around institutions—he is, after all, interested in how the ideological and material contexts of the production of imaginative texts affect the process and products of creative production. (And what is a consideration of the digital environments in which creative writing takes place if not a consideration of ideological and material context?) Recalling that in his first chapter he characterizes what he calls the "institutional conventional wisdom" of creative writing: that creative writing is taught by poets and fiction writers who largely refuse to theorize the cultural, political, and economic ways "creative" work operates. According to the "institutional conventional wisdom," creative writing has largely rejected the academic work of college and university curriculums in order to foster an understanding of the process of composition as "something so individual, intrinsic, even 'mysterious,' [that] it cannot really be analyzed or explained in any significant way" (16). According to Mayers, even the Association of Writing Programs (AWP)—creative writing's major professional organization—reinforces this conventional wisdom. D. W. Fenza, AWP's former executive director, argued in the *Writer's Chronicle*, AWP's official journal, that "the goal of creative writing is to [help students] become, first and foremost, accomplished writers who make significant contributions to contemporary literature. All the other goals, like becoming an academic professional, are ancillary to that artistic goal" (Mayers 19). In the hierarchy Fenza establishes, Mayers points out, placing academic pursuits as they may pertain to creative writing works only to isolate creative writing not only from literary or composition studies, but also from the work of the college or university at large. In this way, creative writing becomes reduced to craft, understood merely as the manipulation of the surface features of a text.

Mayers' argument in *(Re)Writing Craft* (and his call to action in "One Simple Word") works toward framing an understanding of craft as not only the manipulation of the surface features of a text, but also, more importantly, the process of generating a text—enabled by the ideological, material, cultural, and political forces that surround it—that grapples with meaning in a critical and symbolic way. He calls this "craft criticism" and defines it as "an attempt to situate the writing of poetry and fiction, and the teaching of poetry and fiction writing, within institutional, political, social, and economic contexts. As such, many of the concerns of craft critics may be called rhetorical" (34). By recruiting a rhetorical analytical method from composition and rhetoric, Mayers analyzes the ways in which criticism regarding the craft of creative writing has been imagined in the professional journals and organizations that surround the field of creative writing. In short, Mayers works toward framing craft criticism as a form of criticism that foregrounds textual production while backgrounding textual interpretation. While literary criticism uses methods of interpretation to examine the ways in which imaginative literature operates, craft criticism uses methods of production to examine the ways in which imaginative literature operates—and how it can help its authors and audience members engage critically with the cultural environment that surrounds them.

Complicating a tradition of creative writing scholarship devoted to the way in which craft is imagined in the foundational work of scholars like Wendy Bishop and Hans Ostrom (i.e., as a set of—often pedagogically situated— skills for poets, fiction and creative nonfiction writers to master), Mayers's argument builds on the work of scholars like Katherine Haake and Patrick Bizzaro. Haake's book *What Our Speech Disrupts: Feminism and Creative Writing Studies* intervenes at the site of craft in order to theorize the ways in which craft not only mobilizes resistance to hegemonic forces (e.g., through learning and employing craft, writers learn how to speak back to power) but also intervenes at the site of where craft intersects with institutional, cultural, and political forces (e.g., the highly masculinized ways in which "the writer" is often imagined in those contexts). Bizzaro's argument in another essay written for *College English*, "Research and Reflection in English Studies: The Special Case of Creative Writing," makes a case for academically employed creative writers to acknowledge the crucial role their institutions have played in not only what they do, but in who they are. Mayers's take on creative writing studies comes from this line of creative writing scholarship and, as such, is devoted to the deep examination of the forces that circulate through the act of writing creatively in the academy.

This kind of engaged theorizing about creative production, Mayers argues, tends to position craft criticism according to four basic categories: process, genre, authorship, and institutionality. Craft critics investigating questions about *process* engage with concerns regarding whether or not a writer can determine in advance what a particular piece of writing will look like, sound like, or mean. Questions of *genre* deal with definitions and borders (what is poetry?) and questions of *authorship* explore the debate surrounding the intrinsic originality and talents of the writer, while questions of *institutionality* "focus on how the teaching of writing (and reading) is institutionalized within creative writing programs at colleges and universities," exploring how creative writing practices have been shaped by their presence in the academy (47).

Each of these four categories, of course, engages with the digital in some fashion. *Process*: Can a writer determine what a piece of writing will look like as it develops across digital technologies? What happens when poems intersect with songs, video, and image while integrating reader response? *Genre*: Are blogs creative nonfiction? *Authorship*: How have notions of "originality" changed in an open source culture? *Institutionality*: How can scholars in creative writing help parse out and understand the shifting dynamics of print and electronic reading/writing practices as they are presently evolving in the academy at the undergraduate workshop level as well as the PhD and teacher training level? Each of these four criteria directs scholars in creative writing studies toward examinations of the ways in which craft criticism can deepen our understanding of the surface features of a text as well as—when applied to their digital contexts—examinations of the ways in which contextual and technological developments can—and often do—change the process and products of creative production.

I want to organize this digital arm of creative writing studies according to these four categories.[1] When we take into account the ways in which digital technologies have reshaped genres, contexts, and even authors of imaginative texts, I argue that we begin to see the ways in which creative writing can deepen an understanding of how the act of composing is shaped by digital technologies in the twenty-first century as well as a beginning of the broader implications for creative writing's place in the digital humanities. In this chapter I will briefly outline each of these four categories within their digital environments and provide a close examination of how process is redefined with creative writing studies, then extend my examination of the categories of genre, authority/subjectivity, and institutional practice in the subsequent chapters.

Hypertext and its descendents: Digital processes

The implications of digital technologies and ideologies on the act of composing, of course, are nothing new to composition and rhetoric. Even the role of imaginative texts in this thread of scholarship isn't exactly new. In 1998, *Kairos* published a special issue on hypertext fiction and poetry, grappling with a range of pedagogical and theoretical concerns presented through the electronic threading of multiple narratives and themes in short stories, novels, and poetry made possible by hypertext. The issue grappled with the concerns of the time: the pedagogical advantages of using the web to construct e-zines for creative writing classes, the interruption of linearity in the recursive nature of hypertext, and, to a smaller degree, hypertext's visualization of short stories and poems on the development of ways of seeing alongside ways of reading.

The last decade of the twentieth century, in fact, saw a surge in hypertext fiction. Michael Joyce's "Afternoon, A Story," largely considered one of the original hypertext short stories, Douglas Cooper's serialized novel *Delirium*, and Shelly Jackson's "Patchwork Girl" created a space for examining and experimenting with the process of producing imaginary texts across the then emerging technology of the world wide web. Hypertext fiction, borrowing, as Kenneth Goldsmith points out, from a literary tradition of heavily referential high modernist writing (Joyce, Eliot), also steered that tradition in a new direction—one shaped, of course, by the technology used as the storytelling canvas. For example, Jackson's "Patchwork Girl," in which Mary Shelly reinvents the female monster that Victor Frankenstein kills in her novel, plays with notions of form and authorship as well as what it means to write imaginatively when we consider writing as a technology itself. The narrator explains that she is "buried here. You can resurrect me, but only piecemeal. If you want to see the whole, you will have to sew me together yourself." Offering the reader a series of narrative loosely assembled through interlocking links that trace the story into its own body, "Patchwork Girl" comes equipped with nineteenth-century anatomical images of the female body dissected and presented alongside what eventually becomes a love story between the narrator and her creation:

> I had sewn her, stitching deep into the night by candlelight, until the tiny black stitches wavered into script and I began to feel that I was writing, that this creature I was assembling was a brash attempt to achieve by artificial means the unity of a life form—a unity perhaps more rightfully given, not made; continuous, not interrupted; and subject to divine truth, not the will to expression of its prideful author. *Authoress*, I amend, smiling.

Then, later:

> I have a crazy wish! I wish that I had cut off a part of me, something Percy would not miss, but something dear to me, and given it to be a part of her. I would live on in her, and she would know me as I know myself. I fear this, but crave it. I do not know if she would want it. But I could graft myself to that mighty vine. Who knows what strange new fruit the two of us might bear?

Jackson's cyberfeminist narrative points us to the disruptive way in which a recursive text, such as hypertext, literally bears new fruit in its ability to offer alternatives to linear narrative (which are largely, of course, imagined as masculinized narratives) as well as how new bodies—texts—develop across new means for writing those bodies. That is to say: Jackson's story is simultaneously informed by the literary tradition it stems from as well as the self-conscious act of writing the tradition across a new technology. Writing, in this way, is presented as another kind of technology, one that could assemble, albeit artificially, "the unity of a life form." Its status as a technology, in other words, is integrated into the process as well as the product, so that something new can be born.[2]

The emergence of hypertext fiction, in many ways, can be seen as the search for such a unity in the midst of rapidly changing technological shifts that creative writers predominantly viewed suspiciously, despite the active publishing of those working with and within hypertext. Shelly Jackson's teacher, Robert Coover, who taught a course on hypertext fiction writing at Brown puts it this way in his essay "The End of Books," published in Wendy Bishop and Hans Ostrom's collection *Colors of a Different Horse*:

> Writing students are notoriously conservative creatures. They write stubbornly and hopefully within the tradition of what they have read. Getting them to try out alternative or innovative forms is harder than talking them into chastity as a lifestyle. But confronted with hyperspace, they have no choice: all the comforting structures have been erased. It's improvise or go home. Some frantically rebuild those old structures, some just get lost and drift out of sight, most leap in fearlessly without even asking how deep it is (infinitely deep) and admit, even as they paddle for dear life, that this new arena is indeed an exciting, provocative, if frequently frustrating medium for the creation of new narratives, a potentially revolutionary space, capable, exactly as advertised, of transforming the very art of fiction even if it now remains somewhat at the fringe, remote still, in these very early days, from the mainstream.

The technologies of the time, while fringe at their outset, developed at a rapid pace. Software platforms like StorySpace—on which most hypertext was written at the end of the twentieth century—became Tinderbox. And the development of web 2.0 technologies compounded the nonlinear and intertextual possibilities inherent in the act of writing imaginatively while also making technological conditions the norm for writers.

In *Hypertext 3.0: Critical Theory and New Media*, George Landow characterizes the developments since hyptertext:

> Some . . . digital applications, genres, and media . . . do not take the specific form of hypertext. Some of these, such as Weblogs, show an important relation to hypermedia, but others, like computer games, have only a few points of convergence with it. Still others of increasing economic, educational, and

cultural importance, such as animated text, text presented in PDF format, and streaming sound and video, go in very different directions, often producing effects that fundamentally differ from hypermedia. (xiii)

As I will discuss toward the end of this section, those differences amount to the critical elements at stake in framing a digital understanding of creative writing studies, but here it is important to illustrate the difference between what Landow's understanding of hyptertext is (a text that connects internally and externally to parallel or contrasting texts) and what I'm referring to as digital or new media (platforms that enable a multimodality that serves to open a text up to a variety of media). Recall that in *The Rhetoric of Cool*, Jeff Rice characterizes this in rhetorical terms: "I recognize that rhetoric and rhetorical invention emerge out of a number of influences: art, film, literature, music, record covers, cultural studies, imagery, technology, and, of course, writing" (10). Likewise, imaginative invention emerges from (at least) the same set of influences, and creative writing's challenge, as I see it, is similar: to foreground this influence on our understanding of craft, particularly as all those influences Rice describes above exist in our often-trafficked digital writing spaces.

Scholarship in literary studies and composition and rhetoric has since followed the development of hypertext to new media to exciting places, inviting us, as N. Katherine Hayles does, to consider the "medial ecology" in which reading and writing take place daily in the twenty-first century, pointing out that "computer screens [are] being arranged to look like television screens, television screens with multiple windows made to look like computer screens, print books mimicking computers, computers being imaged to look like books" (5). The complex ecology in which Hayles plunges her argument in *Writing Machines* asks a fundamental question that has helped propel a new direction for literary study: How does the materiality of the digital age affect the literary artifact? As Rice generates rhetorical tropes made possible only by virtue of their digital roots in *The Rhetoric of Cool*, Hayles helps generate an understanding of literary study that takes into account the (per)mutations made possible in an age of electronic writing.

With few exceptions, like Coover's hypertext workshop and the flurry of hypertext short stories and poems published rapidly through the 1990s, scholarship in creative writing didn't pick up on these interests as enthusiastically as these two threads of English studies did. However, poets, fiction and creative nonfiction writers did.[3] While most MFA programs continued to provide workshop-based pedagogical methods and print-based praxes and practices, the web saw a rush of creativity in the form of online literary journals, blogs, and multimedia projects. And while *Kairos* developed its "Inventio" section, which is devoted to "the decisions, contexts, and contributions that have constituted a particular webtext . . . . Authors include, alongside or integrated with their finished webtexts, materials that help them articulate how and why their work came into being" (which is arguably a proto-digital-craft-criticism), creative writers experimented with how digital technologies redefine the boundaries we draw around fiction, poetry, and creative nonfiction. How a text changes across emergent technologies is now, as a result, something we can look back on and examine in terms established through the *process* category of digital craft criticism.

To see this development, it helps to notice how print adapted to a readership that became equipped with a technological way of reading fostered by immersion in the internet and web 2.0 culture. As Hayles discusses in *Writing Machines*, Mark Danielewski's 2000 novel *House of Leaves* infamously borrows a visual template from digital writing in not only the formatting of that novel— the text visually reframes different genres (primarily fiction and journalism) in its treatment of "The Navidson Record" (the text's central account of the physically impossible house that the novel's central characters, the Navidson family, document in their home footage)—but also every time the word "House" appears in the text it is in blue as if a link in a hypertext story. The novel is framed twice: it has a forward by Johnny Truant who discovers a text about a family that bought a house and became consumed by its physical properties written by a recently deceased author named Zampanò. The novel is immersive in a narrative fashion—Truant supplies the reader with Zampanò's original text outfitted with Truant's own footnotes and explanations—and readers are asked to occupy a worlding effect that allows the story of the Navidson family to refract through multiple layers that present as much of a multimedia environment as print can make possible. The novel is ultimately about the broken up film footage (a visual medium) of the house, written up by Zampanò (in various notes, texts, and interviews and newspaper clippings) and commented on by Johnny Truant, who discovered Zampanò's notes and unfinished narrative following his death. A full-length companion album, released by the musician Poe, provides an aural dimension to the novel as well. Titled *Haunted*, Poe's album loosely references the novel and, likewise, the novel references the album and lyrics found in particular songs.

What's interesting for our purposes is the way we see Danielewski's novel engage with other media. As Hayles points out, the novel is brought to its medium's limit. Kodwo Eshun, in *More Brilliant Than the Sun: Adventures in Sonic Fiction*, argues that the digital practices in hip-hop and electronic music have developed to the point of amplified integration, contributing to the birth of a new audio paradigm that integrates sound, vision, and bodies. In this paradigm traditional categories breakdown—songs can become fiction and fiction can become songs—and a large part of Eshun's project is capturing the movement and kinetics of aesthetic practice in the twenty-first century. As he puts it:

> You are not censors but sensors, not aesthetes but kinaesthetes. You are sensationalists. You are the newest mutants incubated in womb-speakers. Your mother, your first sound. The bedroom, the party, the dancefloor, the rave: these are the labs where 21st C nervous systems assemble themselves, the matrices of the Futurrhythmachinic Discontinuum. The future is a much better guide to the present than the past. (001)

By breaking down the language into a kind of cyberpoetics, Eshun's manifesto points us toward the interaction of texts across multiple media platforms—an integration of story as it becomes intensified and experienced through sound, images, and text. When put next to a born-digital, multimedia, interactive, episodic novel like *Inanimate Alice*, Danielewski's and Eshun's work shows us the ways in which imaginative narrative has begun to develop across emergent technologies. The role of the visual and aural, integral to the narrative of Danielewski's *House of Leaves* and the argument of Eshun's manifesto, is also part of the fundamental composition of *Inanimate Alice*, which is designed (a word I use here deliberately) for long-term literacy development across years of reading. *Inanimate Alice*, in the words of its creators, novelist Kate Pullinger and digital artist Chris Joseph, is a "transmedia project, designed at the outset as a story that unfolds over time and on multiple platforms." A hybrid of fixed storytelling and embedded game playing, *Inanimate Alice* is about a young woman named Alice and her imaginary friend Brad, an avatar she and the reader use in the coming-of-age story that *Inanimate Alice* becomes: in the digital novel, Alice eventually fulfills her calling as a video game designer. Through a network of aural, visual, and language-oriented texts, readers work alongside, sometimes as, Alice as she grows up. George Landow called this sort of storytelling a "read-write system," arguing along poststructuralist lines that "open" systems like hypertext and, I would add here, digital writing (as opposed to the "closed" systems of print technologies), "offer students . . . a laboratory with which to test [poststructuralism's] ideas" (2). *Inanimate Alice* is just such a laboratory, not just *inviting* readers to imagine themselves as both reader and writer set afloat in Roland Barthes' "galaxy of signifiers," but now *requiring* them to be.

To consider our question regarding process (can a writer determine in advance what a particular piece of writing will look like, sound like, or mean?) in a digital environment, then, is to consider the relationship a writer's imaginative text establishes with its reader and the role new media play in the development of that relationship. In the case of digital imaginative texts, no longer is reading exclusively an act of interpretation. It requires, in a literal and material fashion, participation as well. To determine the narrative is simple enough (even in *Inanimate Alice* there is a kind of determinative linearity in effect), but how a writer crafts that narrative will require the skillful deployment of particular technologies that provide sensory immersion. Digital environments provide immersive multimodality and worlding features that are dependent on an affective ambient world of integrated sound, image, and text, each of which requires integrated as well as independent theorization. Because digital imaginative texts require participation they require an understanding of how craft synthesizes texts and readers. Brian Massumi, in *Parables for the Virtual*, calls this "actualizing" the digital. If imaginative writers wish to sandwich their readers into their texts by integrating into those texts readers' sensory participation (as interactive digital storytelling allows), then one consideration that the *process* category of digital creative writing studies brings to light is the need to develop a sustained theoretical approach toward the sensory and interpretive immersion that craft becomes. While the figure of reader-as-writer is hardly new to scholarship, the recruitment of technologies that materially require the reader to occupy/construct that duality is. Creative writing studies in the twenty-first century can use the digital environment in which this duality takes places as a way of asking imaginative writers to begin examining/imagining writing beyond the sensation provided by lines of language on the page and how participation with a variety of sensation may provide new ways of understanding craft as a synthesis of readers' affect and participation in an unfolding narrative.

Genre(s) growing

Ander Monson's 2010 book *Vanishing Point: Not a Memoir* helps us begin to see more specifically what the *genre* category of craft criticism looks like as it matures in the digital age. "This is a book," he writes on the first page. "It is fixed in time, in space, in print, an artifact." But his "brain, of course, is flux, motion, synapses, connecting and reconnecting and thinking exploding everywhere" (1). So he has employed footnote-like "daggers," which, he explains, "lead to things that exceed the capacity of footnotes. Some of them have video. Some images. Some evolving text" (2). The daggers take you to Monson's website. The subtitle of the book urges readers not to read it as a memoir, but (as we see develop in the book) rather as an interrogation of the "I" the memoirist recruits, which, of course, requires Monson to write some autobiography and allows the alchemy of digital and print technologies to challenge that autobiography. The result is a kind of imaginative text that we might call "creative nonfiction," but one that grapples in a sophisticated way with the possibilities afforded a poet, novelist, or essayist (Monson is all three) who engages with generic conventions in a digital environment. Heir to the hypertext, *Vanishing Point* picks up on how memoir can recruit digital tools to redefine "craft" and to change a memoir into—for lack of a word that has yet to emerge from the ether—"not a memoir." *Vanishing Point* is "not a memoir," after all, because the tools Monson employs—print as well as video, image, and sound—often veer his book away from him, allowing a sort of flexibility with the memoir form that disperses the "self" he interrogates as a way of keeping the book in perpetual motion, sometimes getting away from himself (there are strange histories that leak out of the book and into the web) and sometimes returning to himself (as he does when he describes his childhood or his experience with jury duty).

More specifically, *Vanishing Point* includes an essay titled "Solipsism." This essay was originally written not just on, but for, Monson's own website. As a result the essay, of course, grew, accumulating footnotes and other "paraphernalia," and one of the later additions to the essay describes the "life" of the essay after it was published on Monson's website:

> So the best thing about this essay—and the website containing it that functions as its own venue for publication, which has both good and bad qualities—is that after being composed and published here *(strand one)*, it was picked up by this great newish magazine *The Pinch*, being a cool magazine, formerly *River City*, out of University of Memphis. They did a great print version of it *(strand two)* with some serious design elements that make for a very interesting and provocative read. I find out today (04.16.08) that it will be reprinted in *The Best American Essays 2008*, being *strand three* of the same essay. Or perhaps *strand* is wrong. Maybe it is *strain*, like something viral and expanding. All of this brings up a number of interesting questions: one is how the design elements of the piece will be translated to the *BAE* format, and how much say I will get in the process. If design means, and in this essay (particularly in the version printed in *The Pinch*) it certainly does, then modifying the design means meaning changes. So I would hope that I will get to tinker. (otherelectricities.com/neckdeep/ solipsism.com)

So an "un"-memoir about "the self" in twenty-first-century American culture becomes not only an example of how one can write about "the self" in the digital age, but also a commentary on the institutional ways (in this case, the institution is the *Best American* series) in which conforming genre to print-based conventions of that genre alters the meaning of the piece. But, of course, Monson's book is just that: a book. Recalling Rice's acknowledgment that invention emerges from a variety of influences—print and digital technologies being two influences now afforded creative writers—it's important to note that *Vanishing Point* asks us to (perhaps paradoxically) reimagine narrative structure beyond the exclusively print-based understanding of that word *and that print will always be one force available to the creative writer*. In this way, we will always be able to identify genres as they emerge and reconfigure across developing technologies; however, a digital understanding of the *genre* prong of craft criticism allows us a point of entry regarding the quality and nature of the interactions of those technologies on the conventions of the texts they produce. In Monson's case, we see the ideological baggage of a print-based understanding of "essay" exert itself on the fact that he was not, in the end, allowed to tinker. And the result was an essay included in an edition of *Best American Essays* that ends up going without an integral part of what that essay is about: its capacity to solipsistically grow and reference itself.

We see similar print-based ideological baggage associated with short stories that appear on Twitter. When Rick Moody published "Some Contemporary Characters" through the online literary magazine *Electric Literature*'s Twitter platform he told *Future Perfect Publishing* that "it felt more like writing haiku" and in Jennifer Egan's tweeted short story "Black Box," (published through *The New Yorker*'s Twitter platform) readers saw a character from her print novel *A Visit From the Goon Squad* return in serialized "mental dispatches" sent from a secret mission that the protagonist, essentially, tweets about[4] ("Rick Moody's Novel Experiment"). The 140-character limit shapes the narrator's dispatches into small lessons she learns while on that secret mission (to seduce and attempt to kill a violent political leader), turning what Egan called a story into a serialized series of observations of a fictional narrative. One of the reader's responses to Egan's story, posted to *The New Yorker*'s website, came from a mildly disgruntled fan: "I'm sorry to inform Ms. Egan that she is writing a narrative poem. I know that sounds very feisty, Venus and Adonis-ish, but I'm convinced that Twitter and short attention spans will be the saving of poetry as a living form" (Egan). In Moody and Egan's cases, writers and readers recruited other genres to help understand the modifications of the genre that surfaced through the interaction of stories and the platform those stories were published through. As Marshal McLuhan argued in *Understanding Media*, any cool medium is going to require the participation of its audience to fully express the potential of that medium—and as we use the vocabulary of (and ideological baggage associated with) print-based understandings of genre to understand how they blur and evolve in digital spaces—the *genre* category of a digital craft criticism points us toward how generic conventions are resisted (as they are in *Vanishing Point: Not a Memoir*) or mutated (as they are in the "live" stories of the tweeted work of Rick Moody and Jennifer Egan). In short, identifying and investigating the ways digitized craft invites the technology to play a role in the contour of the work helps scholars of creative writing studies develop sophisticated understandings of the ways genres blur and mature through electronic writing practices.

Authors, avatars, and identity: Managing authorship and ownership in a digital age

Perhaps the most developed category of digital creative writing studies published so far has been regarding notions of originality and authorship as they are complicated by electronic writing practices. Jonathan Lethem's 2007 essay "The Ecstasy of Influence: A Plagiarism" (anthologized, as a matter of fact, in the same *Best American Essays* volume as Monson's "Solipsism") addresses the historical lineage of appropriation in the arts, arguing that "art is sourced [and] apprentices graze in the field of culture," ultimately mounting a Bakhtinian position about the ways in which intertextuality in the arts has always been a rich resource, a lifeblood, in fact, for any writer or artist looking to engage and substantively develop the culture around her. In the addendum following the essay, Lethem reveals the sources he "plagiarized" in the writing of his essay—the overwhelming majority of the essay is a collage of other writers' and artists' work. Lethem plagiarizes a complex argument regarding one particular method used often in digital writing practices: appropriation. Digital writing practices, he points out, simply acknowledge it by requiring its use. "Digital sampling is an art method like any other," he claims, "neutral in itself." In *The Rhetoric of Cool*, Rice brings this practice into the precincts of composition studies, addressing the "borrowing" logic present during but absent from composition studies' lynchpin year of 1963: "Appropriation . . . allows [us] to consider what the pedagogical implications of this moment might be for composition studies—how we appropriate and apply appropriations rhetorically to make meaning in technology-rich environments" (51).

Kenneth Goldsmith's *Uncreative Writing: Managing Language in the Digital Age* shows us what this means for creative writing and refers to appropriation practices as "pushing language around" in digital spaces, arguing that these practices—which he also historicizes in a lineage that includes Walter Benjamin, James Joyce, Gertrude Stein, William Burroughs, and Andy Warhol—are capable of emotionally moving audiences and should, therefore, find a sophisticated home in the teaching of imaginative writing. Such a home in the field of creative writing—which he says is "stuck" on perpetuating an incorrect notion of the "original" artist—has been difficult to find because, he argues, creative writing has been reluctant to follow the strides made in other arts and aesthetic theory, particularly music and painting, where appropriation is a commonly used practice.[5] He explains:

> Perhaps one reason writing is stuck might be the way creative writing is taught. In regard to the many sophisticated ideas concerning media, identity, and sampling developed over the past century, books about how to be a creative writer have completely missed the boat, relying on clichéd notions of what it means to be "creative." These books are peppered with advice, like "A creative writer is an explorer, a ground-breaker. Creative writing allows you to chart your own course and boldly go where no one has gone before." Or, ignoring giants like de Certeau, Cage, and Warhol, they suggest that "creative writing is liberation from the constraints of everyday life." (7)

Resisting these clichés, Goldsmith argues, requires invigorating creative writing by addressing the ways digital writing practices—which include, for Goldsmith, not only appropriation (although that's a large part of Goldsmith's argument), but also code writing, collage writing, and performance art—are descendents of the literary avant-garde. Advocating a context-is-the-new-content approach to the understanding of creative writing, Goldsmith proposes what he calls Uncreative Writing: "While traditional notions of writing are primarily focused on 'originality' and 'creativity,' the digital environment fosters new skill sets that include 'manipulation' and 'management' of the heaps of already existent and ever-increasing language" (15). Uncreative Writing develops conceptual, pedagogical, and practical understandings of how to "manipulate" and "manage" the heaps of language in those environments in imaginative ways.

Invited to the White House to read his work in April 2012, Goldsmith read a poem titled "Traffic," a collage of traffic reports from Manhattan. When recontextualized for a White House audience, the poem—not one line of which Goldsmith "wrote"—achieved a poetic accomplishment by not only presenting "gridlock" to an often argued "gridlocked" audience, but more importantly by illustrating the cadences, images, and materiality of everyday language in an elevated context. By "pushing around" traffic reports from the radio to the page to an audience at the White House, Goldsmith's ready-made poetry draws from an aesthetic set in motion by Duchamp, de Certeau, Cage, and Warhol and, as such, is designed to upset conventional models and expectations of what we consider "creative" or "poetry" to be. In this way, much of Goldsmith's argument in *Uncreative Writing* works toward establishing conceptual models of what it means to write imaginatively in the digital age, exemplified perhaps most effectively in the course he teaches (also called "Uncreative Writing") at the University of Pennsylvania in which "students are penalized for showing any shred of originality and creativity. Instead, they are rewarded for plagiarism, identity theft, repurposing papers, patchwriting, sampling, plundering, and stealing" (8).

At stake in Lethem and Goldsmith's arguments are, obviously, notions of what originality means in an open source culture. It's easy to see the ways in which they champion a kind of originality that recruits culture in order to reimagine it.[6] And while these are themselves important issues at stake in how we frame and present notions of "originality" to imaginative writers in creative writing classrooms—and should be followed up on in creative writing scholarship devoted to the *author* category of digital craft criticism—they also help develop notions of authorship that begin to emerge as they do for N. Katherine Hayles and Ander Monson, both of whom use ciphers themselves in their own work as a way of working through the compounding and refracting of what authorship means in digital spaces. In other words, digital writing practices are not only shifting our understandings of plagiarism and originality, they are also helping scholars and creative writers address how authority can be reimagined. Instead of examining creative authorship at the extremes of a spectrum with the individual genius on one end and the death of the author on the other, the *authorship* category of digital craft criticism asks creative writing scholars to imagine the multiplication of the author, an author who can appear in her own webtext, video, embedded image, animation, or print text wearing a variety of masks and playing a variety of roles, all of which work toward a choreographed effect that her imaginative text aims to achieve.

David Shield's book *Reality Hunger: A Manifesto* argues that these concerns go so far as to redefine an audience's relationship with reality. Citing popular culture's dismay at both James Frey and J. T. Leroy's controversial deceptions regarding who they were as opposed to who their audience thought they were,

Shields points out that our culture "turned them into a spectacle" rather than addressed the issues at stake in the issues backgrounding their public lies like, for example, the role their publishers played in asking, even if not directly, to lie in the way that each did—as well as the ways in which a popular culture simultaneously enthralled and repulsed by "reality television" hungers for public figures to believe in and reject, roles that both Frey and Leroy ultimately played out. Shields advocates for the same kind of appropriation and conceptual recontextualization of writing that Lethem and Goldsmith champion (in fact his entire book is plagiarized as well—a collage of over 500 clips of other writers and artists' work), but links his project to a larger cultural argument regarding how those concerns reject *and* recruit deception, citing the industrialization of creative work through the publishing and academic industries as the main force behind policing categories such as fiction and nonfiction and the ways those categories ask authors to occupy different kinds of ethos.[7] When digital writing practices ask (and often require) authors to experiment with the different kinds of author/ity that emerge when hybridizing and modifying genres, then an attendant ethos also needs to emerge. As such, the *authorship* category of digital craft criticism begins the project of (re)imagining the ethos that imaginative writers occupy when appropriating, employing or modifying language, ready-made texts, and/or particular genres.

Institutionality

While Shields considers the shape and regulation of cultural assumptions regarding originality, authority, and ethos, another major concern regarding the ways digital technologies have reshaped creative production, of course, has been in academia's adaptation to electronic reading and writing practices. Collapsing the divide between readers and writers, social media and other digital technologies ask the publishing industry as well as creative writing MFA/PhD programs to consider how institutional practices adapt. Imagining craft as it intersects with institutions and the effects those institutions have on creative production, as a result, will increasingly require examining the ways in which fluid communication between writers and readers and cheaper, easier, and more effective distribution methods—all effects of digital technologies—have modified the practices of those institutions. Put simply: how are colleges and universities adapting their undergraduate, MFA, and PhD programs to these developments? Creative writing, as it works out a more sophisticated understanding of the role digital technologies have played in these developments, must grapple *at least* with how academic institutions are learning to progress in light of the influence of digital technologies.

Some academic institutions are already beginning to position pedagogical concerns to address the opportunities digital technologies provide. Courses like the University of Massachusetts—Amherst's "Experimental Writing Workshop," in which students enroll at the 200 level for a course "designed on the premise that writing can be playful and play can be both creative and productive," provides a loose framework for a rotating set of courses to address a variety of "experimental" concerns, one of which they call "Digital Storytelling" (*The Writing Program*). George Mason University's "Digital Creative Writing" course is a "combined workshop and studio course in technological and aesthetic issues of reading and writing hypermedia texts with emphasis on poetry, fiction, creative nonfiction, mixed genre, drama, or performance" (*English Department*). As creative writing begins to consider its status in the twenty-first century, those who take creative writing seriously must begin to consider how our institutional practices—ranging from the undergraduate workshop to teacher training—frame an understanding of and scholarship regarding how our craft and practices as teachers/writers demands new theorization in light of digital technologies.

In *Establishing Creative Writing Studies as an Academic Discipline*, Dianne Donnelly examines the history of the workshop method and addresses technology in terms of the "digital natives" we teach in our creative writing classrooms:

> How are creative writing educators to connect with students who are preoccupied with a virtual rather than a physical world, students who are more likely to skip university lectures and less likely to go to the library and check out a book? Are our writing students among the average college graduates who have "spent less than 5,000 hours of their lives reading, but over 10,000 hours playing video games (not to mention 20,000 hours of watching TV)," as Marc Prensky (2001) claims in "Digital Natives, Digital Immigrants?" We do know that our students are among the majority who

want technology at the ready. "The more portable the better," Carlson (2005) notes. After all, he suggests, "they are able to juggle a conversation on Instant Messenger, a Web-surfing session, and an iTunes playlist while reading *Twelfth Night* for homework." Are creative writing teachers ready to embrace and prepare for changes that suit these Googlers—to construct workshops online, create videos and modules, craft lectures on podcasts, which can then be downloaded to students' iPods, becoming portable, rewindable, even pauseable? Should they be? (92)

As Goldsmith's course on "Uncreative Writing" at the University of Pennsylvania illustrates, by beginning to try such a connection through the deep theorization and scholarly treatment of the practices we develop in light of digital technologies, creative writing can begin to imagine workshops that not only employ digital technologies (I would, to answer Donnelly's question, emphatically say *yes*, we *should* be embracing the "change that suit[s] these Googlers" but in a cautious and thoroughly theorized way) but also coursework that addresses these concerns in PhD programs that provide candidates the opportunity to engage in the production of knowledge and creative texts that employ the digital as well as the teacher training we conduct (or don't) in those programs. As Kelly Ritter argues in "Professional Writers/ Writing Professionals: Revamping Teacher Training in Creative Writing PhD Programs," the conditions surrounding pedagogical theory/practice as they are employed and investigated through graduate study in creative writing has needed attention for some time. She concludes:

> through the lenses of university public relations officials, graduate recruitment materials, and rare success stories belonging to famous writers who need never teach again. Graduate programs must not continue to allow creative writing to be the riderless horse in the larger field of English studies. (227)

Investigations into the *institutionality* of a digital craft criticism is a way of imagining what is at stake in our digital considerations and conceptions of craft as they are inflected through their (re)production in workshops and teacher training. To build off Goldsmith's course: to provide undergraduate creative writers with coursework through which to investigate and practice creative writing as appropriation (or any other digital writing practice) requires that we incorporate into our teacher training in creative writing *how* and *why* we position students in these contexts in the first place.

Craft and contours: English studies and digital craft criticism

In his book *Literary Art in Digital Performance*, editor Francisco Ricardo investigates how literature changes when digital technology is used for aesthetic reasons and not just distribution. In his introduction, he argues:

> While human expressive force remains vibrant, electronic media have made it possible to create work that spans traditional distinctions at key junctures, to include the aesthetic and the poetic; the entirely participatory and the entirely receptive; the act of narrative creation and that of real-time production. (2)

While Ricardo's book works toward a literary criticism devoted to examining "the cinematic element in video games, poems in projective installations, dramatic reenactments played out in simulated online worlds [and] the audible immersive [that is] explorable in open physical space," the interests in his book certainly line up with how creative texts (and, I would urge, creative writing) begin to illustrate a distinction that emerges in a culture that employs electronic media: namely, the difference between "the entirely participatory and the entirely receptive" (Ricardo 5). An emerging digital understanding of craft criticism unpacks precisely what creative writing studies would be able to examine at a moment in our scholarship when we seem situated somewhere in the middle. Digital understandings of craft will develop alongside—in many cases out of—print forms and perhaps begin to contribute to larger discussions regarding craft and authorship in an age of "participatory" aesthetics, including the ways in which creative writing may begin, eventually, the project of unhinging genre, process/practices, and even authors from their print-based conventions.

Particularly important to imagining craft as a digital immersion and not just a textual surface is the possibility for recruiting (and advocating for further) research devoted to understanding the sensual and affective ways knowledge circulates through the act of reading, viewing, listening, and reacting to imaginative texts. As research in composition studies emerges regarding the ways in which sound, image, and speech complicate the rhetorical and composing situation, creative writing studies needs to begin the important work of thoroughly attending to the particular opportunities afforded by imaginative writers who work at the intersection of storytelling and new media. Digital craft criticism imagines what choices made at the material level contribute not only to the interpretation of the text that requires reading, watching *and* listening, but, more importantly, the limits and horizons that particular material conditions in digital environments make possible for imaginative texts.

Returning to his 2009 article in *College English*, "One Simple Word," Tim Mayers observes that creative writing studies "may harbor the roots of an institutional compromise in which the union between composition and literature does not involve one side winning and the other side losing, but rather both enterprises being transformed [by creative writing studies] so that they can meet on heretofore unimagined ground." Since those roots are spreading into digital ground, it only makes sense that such a union be able to adequately attend to the ways in which the ideological, material, and institutional forces at work on the act of imaginative composition in digital spaces provide one particular way to reinforce that union.

To build a kind of criticism that foregrounds textual production as it engages with digital environments requires the attention to and complication of print-based ways of understanding imaginative texts *as well as* the development of how the digital environs of an imaginative text affect the process of constructing that text. The union that Mayers forecasts in "One Simple Word" emerges strikingly when we consider the effects of digital technologies on conceptions of craft. We can also begin to address a range of research directions—bigger than craft—that require further examination across such an "unimagined ground": the effects of digital research methods on writing novels, short stories, poems, and creative nonfiction, the evolving relationship between video games and narrative structure, the relationship between rhetorical ethics and citizenship as they are imagined and critiqued across "democratizing" stages like online literary journals and in cultural studies scholarship, not to mention the sustained analysis of the cultural, economic, and material ways in which the publishing industry grapples with the digital age, to name only a few. In this way, creative writing studies stands ready to better understand and assess the ways in which a creative writer's work is enabled and limited by her capacity to engage with the opportunities afforded by her, whether in print or digital tradition, or both, asking her to compose through and speak back to traditions both literary and rhetorical as they are preserved and always reimagined.

Notes

1   And while most of the examples I will use in this argument focus on narrative and/or fiction, there are other examples in poetry that require further analysis on behalf of scholars working in creative writing studies. As a scholar focusing primarily on fiction and narrative I am more familiar with these examples and have chosen to use them here.

2   Mark Bernstein, Carolyn Guyer, and Mark Amerika, among others, were actively publishing hypertext work at this time. For more on the specific history of hypertext, see Astrid Ensslin's *Canonizing Hypertext: Explorations and Constructions.*

3   Dianne Donnelly's introduction in *Does the Writing Workshop Still Work?* mentions some of the work being done in the "digital writing workshops" at University of Massachusetts—Amherst, Texas A & M, and George Mason University; however, Donnelly's collection was published in 2010 and illustrates how technology is still only beginning to enter into our considerations of creative writing studies.

4   *A Visit From the Goon Squad* also includes a chapter written in PowerPoint, demonstrating a fluidity on Egan's part regarding the variety of platforms across which story can develop.

5   This practice is also becoming more popular in composition studies. Rebecca Moore Howard's "patchwriting," which she defines as "a method of composing in which writers take the words of other authors and patch them together with few or no changes," examines the borders we use to define plagiarism in the teaching of writing and the ways we can explore those borders in order to help students identify not only the sound practice of intertextuality, but also the critical intervention imperative to great writing.

6   For more on this see Lethem's "Promiscuous Materials Project" on his website. The Project is devoted to fair-trade use of intellectual property, providing writers and artists with materials meant to be appropriated and reused.

7   See also John D'Agata and Jim Fingal's *The Lifespan of a Fact.*

3

Ideology, Subjectivity, and the Creative Writer in the Digital Age

In their 1989 article "The Cultural Politics of the Fiction Workshop," Donald Morton and Mas'ud Zavarzadeh argue that

> the fiction workshop is not a "neutral" place where insights are developed, ideas/advice freely exchanged, and skills honed. It is a site of ideology: a place in which a particular view of reading/writing texts is put forth and through this view support is given to the dominant social order. By regarding writing as "craft" and proposing realism as *the* mode of writing, the fiction workshop in collaboration with humanist critics fulfills its ideological role in the dominant academy by preserving the subject as "independent" and "free." (161, original italics)

Referring to Raymond Carver's minimalist or "dirty realist" influence on creative writing programs in the late eighties and early nineties, Morton and Zavarzadeh's article argues that this way of reading/writing texts perpetuates patriarchal forces and bourgeois economics that, ultimately, turn the fiction workshop into a politically and culturally oppressive space—all in the guise of "freedom" and "voice." "Freedom," after all, is just another ideological construct and they argue that fiction workshops, although claiming to be spaces where students are "free" to discover their voice and develop their individual talent, actually serve ways of reading/writing texts that are monolithic and undertheorized, turning creative writing students into replicated automatons, all reaching for the same aesthetic goals. In other words, fiction workshops don't provide students any space to interrogate the "free" subjectivities that workshop claims to enable. And because of this, creative writers, along the lines of Morton and Zavarzadeh's argument, graduate from creative writing programs as cogs in a capitalistic wheel, writers merely trying to hawk their goods in a market that has decided literary realism is the only important aesthetic project. It is just so tragic, according to this argument, to see so many great minds destroyed by the lack of opportunity to interrogate the "freedom" their creative writing programs provided.[1]

I point this article out not because I disagree—they actually make several important points even if they do overstate the role critical theory should play in creative writing programs—but because they provide a starting point for imagining the ideologies and subjectivities we produce in our workshops. In an era of creative writing practice and scholarship that has largely widened beyond the realist project Morton and Zavarzadeh reference to include digital interests (Donnelly, Mayers, Goldsmith) what subjectivities do we see our practice and scholarship (re)producing? If we look at the ideology and subjectivity Morton and Zavarzadeh claim we reproduce in creative writing classrooms—stable modernist selves, rational, deliberative, and instrumental in their approach toward language—we can see a starting point for what it means to reimagine those selves at the start of the twenty-first century. Or, put another way: What humanist values are relevant to digital creative writing studies, a line of scholarship that, as this chapter will point out, in many ways extends the project of posthumanity, especially as the field of composition studies has imagined it?

In this chapter, I examine the ideological repercussions and student writer subjectivities at stake in creative writing studies' digital turn. As Kenneth Goldsmith points out in *Uncreative Writing*, popular notions of "creativity," notions nearly synonymous with the kind of "freedom" Morton and Zavarzadeh find problematic, must be broken down in our technological age:

> Living when technology is changing the rules of the game in every aspect of our lives, it's time to question and tear down clichés [about creativity] and lay them out on the floor in front of us, then reconstruct these smoldering embers into something new, something contemporary, something— finally—relevant. (9)

What happens to student subjectivity when creative writing tears down its clichés rooted in print-based ideologies and begins the work of reimagining creative writing in the digital age? What is at stake for this emerging discipline and how can we insure that it is in the best interest of our students? How can we use the opportunity to imagine the ways in which creative writing must grapple with the digital as an opportunity to imagine the ways we shape the writers who emerge from our classrooms? In taking these questions on, I aim to reclaim the creative writing classroom as a space where we can begin the project of not only accounting for the ways print-based practices and theories intersect with screen-based (or digital) practices and theories, but also how that intersection affects our students. How do we, in other words, understand the smoldering embers of our postmodern and digital subjectivities? Can we remake them into something relevant?

The "Big T" Text and the "little t" text

In a 300-level undergraduate fiction workshop, I recently found myself navigating a heated discussion about the ways short stories as print artifacts encounter the digital artifacts found so regularly in our lives. We were workshopping a story in which the main character—a socially awkward misfit who yearns for the capacity to connect with his peers while entirely alienating them—communicated mostly through texts, tweets and Facebook status updates. Instead of dialogue, most of the communication between characters came through screen-based mediums and the writer was trying to figure out the best way to make the page mimic the screen. The story, indebted a bit to Tao Lin's digitally soaked short stories and novels, was more or less a traditional short story, driven by a three-part narrative structure (as opposed to being made up of only the tweets and texts themselves), was broken up by the texts and tweets throughout, and was positively received by a classroom filled with students eager to criticize what they saw as the vacuous and shallow form of communication that is texting and tweeting. But as the workshop chugged along, while students addressed the specific ways texts and tweets worked well for humanizing the main character and illustrating his social paralysis, I noticed a young man, ordinarily engaged and vocal in class, staring out the window with a blank stare.

"What do you think?" I asked him.

"About what?"

"The story. These comments on this character."

His answer surprised me. He said that he just didn't think texting and tweeting had any place *in a short story*. None of the short stories he had read ever bothered to concern themselves with technology, something he saw as so momentary, so fleeting that it had no real place in a form meant to stabilize and, ultimately, preserve human experience. Forget about the excellent work done in science fiction, the short stories of Ray Bradbury or Philip K. Dick. That was genre fiction. As Morton and Zavarzadeh would have observed, this student was revealing his privileging of literary realism. Human experiences with technology simply didn't count and so writing about them in a short story disqualified that short story from serious discussion. What actually surprised me most about his response (his genre snobbery isn't anything new) was how rooted in print culture it was. Print culture didn't bother with digital culture. Print culture was about dramatic human experience: mortality, war, love, political upheaval, the meaning of life. Print culture was high-brow. Tweets and texts and technology were about hooking up with friends, sharing pictures, and showing off. Digital culture was decidedly low-brow. Most importantly, though, print culture had become so normalized for him that he couldn't imagine print as a technology itself.

This ideological stance carries with it several implications. Most obviously, it sets up a binary between print and electronic texts. This student was willing to adhere to the ideological way of reading/writing that says print texts are worthy of our attention while electronic texts are not. Turning again toward Kenneth Goldsmith's *Uncreative Writing*, we can see that much of the aesthetic theory that emerged in the mid-twentieth century has emphasized the materiality of language. His argument in *Uncreative Writing* is to build a theory for writing that uses preexisting language in order to fashion poetry and other imaginative texts. This theory, which Goldsmith lines up in a lineage of print writers and visual artists including Gertrude Stein, James Joyce, Vladimir Nabokov, William Burroughs, Asger Jorn, Guy Debord, and Andy Warhol (among many others), emphasizes the opacity of language, its status as not only symbolically significant, but also physically manageable, something writers and artists can repurpose:

> Two movements in the middle of the twentieth century, concrete poetry and situationism, experimented with sliding the slider [of language] all the way up to 100 percent opacity. In uncreative writing, new meaning is created by repurposing preexisting texts. In order to work with text this way, words must

first be rendered opaque and material. Both movements viewed materiality as primary goals, the situationists through *detournement* and the concretists by literally treating letters as building blocks. The situationists worked in a variety of mediums, realizing their vision of the city as canvas whereas the concretists took a more traditional tact, mostly publishing books. By envisioning the page as a screen, the concretists anticipated the way we would work with language in the digital world half a century later. (36)

Concretists—a community of artists devoted to playing with the ways language physically occupies our environment in street signs, store fronts, magazines, newspapers, etc.—grew a theoretical framework for their art through experimenting with collage and nonlinear texts that incorporated visual and aural arts. These projects required a manipulation of language that required using language in a material fashion. And as Goldsmith points out above: they wrote books. They saw print as a technology for them to engage: an interface.

What's interesting to note here—and what Goldsmith begins to point his reader toward in the above quote—is the way this forecasts our "management" of language in the digital age. In other words, print is itself treated as a technology, one with material products that can be used themselves as the material for art. As Goldsmith also points out in his argument, this sort of aesthetic theory has largely been normalized in other arts—especially music where appropriation is considered a classical part of the musician's education—but has been slow to gain traction in writing. Until, according to Goldsmith, creative writers entered the digital age.

Digitally born genres of creative writing, of course, appear all over the cultural landscape. As mentioned in the previous chapter, Rick Moody and Jennifer Egan have both published short stories through Twitter. Narrative Magazine (which exists only online) regularly publishes what they call "iStories," flash fiction pieces limited to 150 words. Ander Monson's *Vanishing Point: Not a Memoir* uses its footnotes to alert readers to search those terms on the book's website, tumbling readers into a variety of other media (videos, songs, other texts) that literally link that print artifact—a book—to its digital counterpart—the internet. In her book *Toward a Composition Made Whole*, Jody Shipka alerts compositionists to the extreme ways in which new media and our digital moment have been treated in popular mythologizing and our scholarship, reminding us that "literacy has always been multimodal," and that to privilege a text as "digital" because of its final product's status as an iStory or tweeted poem—whatever—is to discount the simple fact that writers have always been mingling with a variety of mediums in the production of traditional print texts. For example, it's not uncommon for poems and short stories that appear in workshops everyday around the country to have been inspired by—or incorporate—a writer's favorite song, or for a writer to do research through online archives, or for a short story to emerge from the "network of literate practices" strung together by an author borrowing generic conventions from, let's say, crime procedurals on television, in the movies, as well as in popular novels. For Shipka, scholars and teachers of writing must find ways of valuing the multimodality that has always gone into the production of the text, whether that multimodality is present in the final product or not. As Amy Letter puts it in her essay "Creative Writing For New Media," even in the technologically mediated creative writing classroom, "our courses aren't about teaching the technology. When we teach poetry writing, we aren't teaching grammar and syntax. We are teaching an art form that uses grammar and syntax in a variety of ways. . . . We inform them of these tools and methods, and they decide whether and where to use consonance, rhyme, caesura, as they pursue larger creative goals" (180). I'll have more on that later, but what I'm interested in here is that electronic and print reading/writing practices are not as mutually exclusive as convention (or tradition) might want us to believe—and they circulate in the same cultural ecologies.

These considerations for the ways in which print engages the digital and vice versa show us that these two ideological ways of approaching reading/writing practices need not be imagined as mutually exclusive. If we are to look at a creative writing pedagogy in a way that is, as Morton and Zavarzadeh want us to, explicit about the ways in which it perpetuates particular reading/writing practices—and if we want to account for the ways in which digitally inflected understandings of creative writing might work—then we must simply admit that a lot of what we ideologically perpetuate in our workshops will be based in traditions both print and digital. How they challenge and charge each other will be continually shaping our pedagogy. That pedagogy will be continually shaping our students.

In order to investigate that process, in this chapter I turn toward the work of Kenneth Goldsmith, Paul Dawson, Katherine Hayles, and Lester Faigley in order to examine that mutual shaping and what it means for creative writing studies. Each of these authors, as I will show, provide avenues into understanding the status of creative writing programs—their limits and their strengths—and the ways in which that field stands to contribute valuably to both university curriculum and contemporary literature. When the act of writing creatively is imagined as a technologically mediated activity—not necessarily a technologically determined one—I argue, a very clear image of how subjectivity and ideology matter to digital creative writing pedagogy appears. From there, we can continue to address what the later chapters of this book examine: how a technologically mediated understanding of creative writing studies stands to (re)imagine genre and process, which I take up in Chapter 4, as well as institutional practice and further avenues for research, which I discuss in the final chapter.

Voice and unoriginality

In his book *Creative Writing and the New Humanities*, Paul Dawson argues that creative writing stands poised at the beginning of the twenty-first century to be the discipline that graduates public intellectuals who are literate, critical, creative, and responsive to the cultural/political landscape. Through historicizing the rise of creative writing programs in the United States alongside literary theory and criticism concerned with how we define "creative," Dawson's argument sets the stage for imagining what he calls "workshop poetics": the elements of meaning making unique to the creative writing workshop. Pausing on voice and recalling Morton and Zavarzadeh's argument, Dawson also points out that

> voice [as it is understood in the creative writing workshop] is a construct [and] Morton and Zavarzadeh's critique of voice relates to the *creative self expression* model of Creative Writing. This model tends to be most overt in adult education and community writing classes, where it often operates as a therapeutic technology of the self, although such a concept of voice and selfhood also exists for many writers and teachers of writing at the university level. (109)

When voice—one of the major pedagogical components of the workshop—is imagined as a construct in the creative writing classroom itself, we open the door for imagining voice as, to use Dawson's word, a *technology* as well as *a site of ideological construction*, a space in which subjectivity is externalized and assumptions and beliefs conducted by that subjectivity can be examined.

Recall that in *(Re)Writing Craft*, Tim Mayers defines "craft criticism" as a form of "critical prose written by self- or institutionally identified 'creative writers'; in craft criticism, a concern with textual production takes precedence over any concern with textual interpretation" (34). Identifying an emergent scholarship in which creative writers have addressed the creative process, Mayers imagines the workshop as a space where students investigate the sort of concerns that Morton and Zavarzadeh examine: voice as a socially and ideologically constructed production, one that carries with it the everyday assumptions we have about the world and can therefore be a rich site of interpretation. Within the model of creative writing pedagogy that Mayers and Dawson construct, student writing is acknowledged as a site, a "technology," to use Dawson's word, that students learn to examine in order to inform their own choices as fiction writers or poets. It is material.

Kenneth Goldsmith's *Uncreative Writing* largely picks up on this and develops a method for teaching digital creative writing that works against print-based ideologies:

> While traditional notions of writing are primarily focused on "originality" and "creativity," the digital environment fosters new skill sets that include "manipulation" and "management" of the heaps of already existent and ever-increasing language. (15)

Goldsmith's project, in fact, largely sets up a way of imagining writing that privileges the manipulation and management of language found in digital environments, claiming that "never before has language had so much materiality—fluidity, plasticity, malleability—begging to be actively managed by the writer" (25). Such active management, for Goldsmith, not only requires a lineage of what we could call digital creative writing pedagogy as it has emerged from print-based creative writing pedagogy but also requires, perhaps more importantly, the value systems and subjectivities we prescribe to such pedagogies. In his workshop, students

> are penalized for showing any shred of originality and creativity. Instead they are rewarded for plagiarism, identity theft, repurposing papers,

patchwriting, sampling, plundering, and stealing. Not surprisingly, they thrive. Suddenly, what they've surreptitiously become expert at is brought out into the open and explored in a safe environment, reframed in terms of responsibility instead of recklessness. (8)

Digital environments have created access to unprecedented amounts of language, and digital technologies encourage the material manipulation of language. Therefore, according to Goldsmith, a digital creative writing pedagogy would celebrate the kind of reappropriation and context-as-the-new-content approach to constructing an imaginative text that he describes above. Doing so, I contend, requires the sort of ideological examination of style and voice that Morton and Zavarzadeh claimed didn't take place in the 1980s. An imperative part of that project, of course, is the examination of subjectivity—more specifically, technologically mediated subjectivity—of the writer within a technologically mediated understanding of creative writing studies.

Medial ecologies and subject positions

Perhaps the most in-depth examination of such subjectivity is provided by N. Katherine Hayles' book *Writing Machines*, in which she adopts a cipher through which the reader literally interfaces as he engages her argument throughout. When that cipher, Kaye,

> first encountered the desktop computer and understood it could be used to create literary texts, she realized that everything important to her met in the nexus of this material-semiotic object. It called forth the questions that continued to fascinate her about scientific research: what does it mean? Why is it important? It confronted her with the materiality of the physical world and its mediation through the technological apparatus. When used for electronic literature, it gave her the same keen pleasure as the print novels she loved, through different sensory and kinesthetic modalities. (15)

Pursuing the materiality of the physical world leads Kaye to challenge many of the ways literary criticism has defined materiality, especially in an age of multimedia. As a result, she situates print and electronic reading/writing practices in a medial ecology, a cultural environment in which books, technotexts, videos, songs, visual art—simulations print and digital—all contribute to a symbolic network that requires a new kind of material-semiotic theorizing. Writers are, of course, situated within this network and once their reading/writing practices, so her argument goes, take this material-semiotic theorizing into account, new sets of theorizing, practicing, and "being in" writing arise. Goldsmith himself is clearly one such writer and when put next to Kaye it is clear to see that writing in the digital age aims to present language as "a medium and not a transparent interface" (Hayles 43).

For Goldsmith, student subjectivity in a digitally inflected creative writing course amounts to playing with notions of the materiality of language that encourages students to see themselves as "unoriginal," as "managers" of language, and as "plunderers and thieves." In Goldsmith's digital writing workshop, therefore, students are required to examine notions of individual genius, the writer's relation to culture and language, and what the effects of the general reappropriation of texts mean in relation to their own writing. Their subjectivity, in other words, is constructed literally through other voices. And the classroom is their opportunity to address what this means for them as writers. In Hayles' argument, writers interface in much the same way; however, language is not the only element they encounter in their medial ecology. They also write with video, sound, kinesthetic modalities. They may see their work as the material construct of others' voices, but also working as a confluence of media. Writers engage not only print and electronic ideologies, but also ideologies that come from music and "the visual arts, computer games, and programming practices" (Hayles 45). While notions of originality are at stake for writers in Goldsmith's classroom, notions of what could be called a multiconsciousness are at stake for Hayles.

These two modes are the dominant ways of thinking about imaginative writers in a digital age. They have in common the requirement that students become active agents in their construction of texts and that voice be seen as a technology itself, yet they differ in their presentation of the ways in which student writers imagine themselves as "original" or even "creative." In Goldsmith's classroom, students are literally unoriginal—and celebrated for being so. In Hayles's, they are writers who write with media, increasing their capacity for new kinds of originality. A creative writing pedagogy that moves along a digital turn will have to ask: How do subjectivity and ideology inflect each other in creative writing pedagogy?

A mediated writer's subjectivity

Another way to ask that question is: How has subjectivity and ideology in creative writing theory and practice changed since Morton and Zavarzadeh's article? Perhaps the most striking answer provided by digital creative writing points us toward the workshop not as a site that perpetuates a "neutral" understanding of itself and its reading/writing practices, but as a place where students are both creative and uncreative, human and cyborg: a place where writing is seen as our most intimate technology. A place where "what counts" as writing has widened beyond the page.[2] As Goldsmith's theory and pedagogy make obvious, the creative writing classroom is a space where particular subjectivities and ideologies are staked out. The fact that he privileges an electronically mediated one over a print-based one shows that as creative writing begins the project of engaging with the ways in which it is mediated by emerging technologies, a variety of subject positions and ideological perspective are beginning to be carved out.

Any creative writing classroom that uses the digital opportunities afforded writers will place writers within assumptions that the aesthetic act is artificial. This isn't new. How creative writing classrooms ask students to handle those aesthetic choices, though, add new elements to that old theoretical position. The cultural politics, for example, of reappropriation require, as Goldsmith says, a "reframing" of the ethics through which writers "write" in his Uncreative Writing class. While those students learn invaluable ways of imagining how voice is a refraction of other voices, they also construct texts that literally ask them to perpetuate plagiarism. That writer's sense of originality—while theoretically complex—carries a political and cultural project along with it that asks creative writing scholars to examine histories (and not just poetics, if we can separate the two for a moment) of reappropriation. The multimodal medial ecology that Hayles points out, while now including digital manifestations, has a lineage all on its own as well: as Shipka points out, "literacy has always been multimodal." Medieval scribes knew this. William Blake knew this. How does its inclusion in creative writing pedagogy, echoing Mayers, help us value methods of production over methods of interpretation?

These are the questions we position students to answer when we ask them to write in/through/with digital environments. Fifteen years have passed since Morton and Zavarzadeh pointed out that the creative writing classroom is not the "neutral" space where realism is the only reading/writing practice employed. We have seen creative writing pedagogy develop ways of imagining students and student work as technologically determined. What's at stake now is how we imagine the ways that technological determinism stands to liberate them—and open the digital creative writing classroom up to the possibilities of finding new connections with diverse sets of older traditions—while serving complex subjectivities capable of wielding an authority conscious of its own place in history.

Electronic ethos

In *Uncreative Writing*, Kenneth Goldsmith calls his poetics a "post-identity literature," citing postmodern identity politics that call into question the stable modern self for the sake of a heteroglossic and "slippery" self that works through digital spaces. He claims that

> if my identity is really up for grabs and changeable by the minute—as I believe it is—it's important that my writing [reflects] this state of ever-shifting identity and subjectivity. That can mean adopting voices that aren't "mine," subjectivities that aren't "mine," opinions that aren't "mine," political positions that aren't "mine," words that aren't "mine" because, in the end, I don't think that I can possibly define what's mine and what isn't. (84)

For Goldsmith, a writer working across digital spaces and through new processes requires a "technology-fueled postidentity writing practice" that "makes the audience wonder whether the author's identity actually had anything to do with the person who wrote it" (90). This is also the case in Monson's *Vanishing Point*; the "self" at work in that text is both Monson and not, as Hayles's cipher Kaye is both Hayles and not. This paradoxical position of authority while participating in digital practices emerges as symptomatic of the conditions inherent in digital spaces. The interface of digital imaginative writing—images, videos, social media, participatory loops—seems to compound those elements at work on what we would traditionally call "an author." What questions does the ideological position required in such a subjectivity require answering?

In the October 5, 2015 issue of *The New Yorker*, Kenneth Goldsmith's "slippery" navigation of what is and isn't his had a particularly problematic effect. Alec Wilkinson's article on the event, "Something Borrowed," walks the reader through the narrative behind Goldsmith's poetics and the conceptual framework he built in order to frame "Uncreative Writing." In describing this poetics, Wilkinson refers to Marjorie Perloff's description of Goldsmith's work: "Perloff's term for Goldsmith's type of writing is 'moving information', by which she means both taking words from one place and using them in another, and the quality produced by the result. A modern writer, operating what Goldsmith calls 'a writing machine', is more a collagist than a writer in the customary sense." Wilkinson also points out that Perloff "regards Goldsmith as 'basically a realistic writer who gives you the feel of what it is like to be living in New York now.'" The duplicity in what he says, though, is problematically compounded at a 2015 reading:

> Last March, Goldsmith gave a reading at a conference at Brown University. He read a poem that he called "The Body of Michael Brown," an appropriation of Brown's autopsy report. . . . About a hundred people were in the audience. Goldsmith wore a long black skirt over dark leggings and a black suit jacket. He looked like a Coptic priest. He stood beneath a projection of a photograph of Brown in his high-school graduation robe. He announced that he would read a poem about the quantified self, meaning one that catalogued the evidence obtained from the close examination of a body. . . . He read for thirty minutes, pacing forward and back. For dramatic effect, he ended with the doctor's observation that Brown's genitals were "unremarkable," which is not the way the autopsy report ends, and when he finished he sat down in the front row. He thought that the reading had been powerful—"How could it not have been, given the material?" he said. He believed he had demonstrated that conceptual poetry could handle inflammatory material and provoke outrage in the service of a social cause. Mairéad Byrne, a poet who heard him, told me that she thought the audience was stunned. A young man in the audience told her that for thirty minutes he had thought about nothing but Michael Brown.

Perloff's description of Goldsmith as a "realistic" writer as well as one who is firmly entrenched in digital poetics brings into relief at least one problematic way in which print and digital ideologies clash: the reappropriation of Michal Brown's autopsy report *as poetry*, the "management" of his "quantified self," results in what many critics and poets have called another violence perpetuated on Michael Brown. While on the one hand, Goldsmith's poem is literally as "real" as language gets—it is an official document at the center of a very heated, polarizing, and political event; the death of a young black man by a white police officer who later resigned as a result of the event—and so can be considered a kind of poetic realism, it is also an effect of Goldsmith's reappropriation logic that his work reframes Brown's body as well as his death. That is, the contexts surrounding Michael Brown's death are the cultural, social, and political conditions that contribute to the perpetuation of violence against black Americans and institutional racism, a highly complex rhetorical terrain. Goldsmith arguably erased those conditions when he "managed" the literal information of Brown's autopsy into the context of a poetry reading. Later in his article, Wilkinson points out:

> A poet named Ken Chen, the executive director of the Asian American Writers' Workshop, wrote that the reading showed that "Conceptual Poetry literally sees itself as white power dissecting the colored body." What seemed to offend people most about Goldsmith's reading was that he appeared to have used Michael Brown's death for his own purposes.
>
> Some people wondered whether the reading might have been received differently if Goldsmith had explained his intentions. If he had "prefaced the work calling it a piece of protest poetry (or something) I am pretty certain the work would have been considered a triumph," Rin Johnson wrote to me. Goldsmith said that he had not made any prefatory remarks because he believed that his sympathies were plain, and because he felt that art should not depend for its effect on explanations.

What are the rhetorical and ethical roles that digital/print practices—and their ideological implications on subjectivity—play in creative writing studies? If the interface is a participant in the production of meaning—interfaces such as software, websites, pages, and audiences—as Goldsmith claims and as his poetry allows (remember, he claims not to "write" anything, since there is already so much written; he simply "moves" it around; it is part of his environment), then does creative writing studies—specifically a digitally inflected understanding of creative writing studies—have ethical imperatives to consider in the ideological stances it takes regarding the study and teaching of its central object of study (the process of producing an imaginative text) as well as the writers it produces?

Lester Faigley, in *Fragments of Rationality: Postmodernity and the Subject of Composition,* positions such questions for composition studies according to its historical development alongside postmodernism, a parallel that he finds interesting because of composition studies' simultaneous rejection and reflection of postmodernism. "Many of the fault lines in composition studies," he argues, "are disagreements over the subjectivities that teachers of writing want students to occupy" (17). Those subjectivities, in Faigley's argument, breakdown according to the degree of autonomy writing teachers want to imagine on the part of their students. Composition studies, in Faigley's understanding of it, is an essentially conservative field, urging students to adopt rational, deliberative, high Enlightenment selves. Citing scholarship in composition that champions "authentic voice" in student writing, Faigley applies postmodern theory to reach an understanding of a kind of disingenuousness at work in such an idea: "To ask students to write authentically about the self assumes that a unified consciousness can be laid out on the page. That the self is constructed in socially and historically specific discursive practices is denied" (127). More specifically, citing bell hooks, Faigley reminds us what having multiple voices in that space between composition studies and creative writing has brought to light:

> Hooks, in *Talking Back,* describes experiences in college creative writing classes where she was told by white teachers and peers that she was using her "true, authentic voice" when she wrote in a particular southern black dialect. She says she was troubled by these comments because she was aware that black poets were capable of speaking in many voices. She then remarks: "The insistence on finding one voice, one definitive style of writing and reading one's poetry, fit all too neatly with a static notion of self and identity that was pervasive in university settings" (11). Hooks gives a powerful example of how the belief in unified subjectivity collapses differences into singular categories of substance—that a black writer's "authentic" voice could be rendered only in a black English dialect. (18)

One of the demanding questions Goldsmith's reading at Brown asks creative writing scholars to investigate is the degree to which the field is actively (re) producing subjectivities that work toward the often political and cultural ends that writers attempt to achieve through aesthetic means. What does it mean for a creative writer to write through multiple voices or to write through voices not his own? This is, for creative writing studies, especially a digital arm of creative writing studies, another way to examine the tension between academic and nonacademic understandings of its object of study. As it was of concern to Peter Elbow, Donald Murray, and Ken Macrorie, the student writer's status as a subject both within and without the university structure, so it must be of concern for creative writing scholars that we systematically examine the subject positions creative writing pedagogy positions creative writing students to occupy. What subjectivities do print and digital ideologies ask students to occupy? Why position them in this way?

This is especially pertinent, I argue, for creative writing, given that arguably, the subjectivity produced is one that is often called upon to play a provocative role in her society. One of art's—and of course, literary art's— goals is at least to reflect a culture and its problems back to itself. And to be able to do so from a variety of perspectives (as hooks remind us). Morton and Zavarzadeh claim that in the 1980s writers in MFA programs primarily learned how to write a genre of literary expression that sold well in a public marketplace. As we can see, creative writing has moved along considerations of its own materiality that has largely led us to a point where we can begin to consider that materiality's effect on the work and the writers our field produces. In other words, an "academic creative writer" can be seen along a spectrum where on one end is Morton and Zavarzadeh's bourgeois writer and on the other is Goldsmith's politically active and culturally problematic one. To write in digital environments, as Goldsmith shows, is problematic in particular sociopolitical ways. Writers are supposed to upset the status quo. And is this what Goldsmith did? In a field such as creative writing, are the subjectivities we aim to produce supposed to be problematic from the start? That is to say: are the subjectivities that creative writing pedagogies produce inherently countercultural? Or are there "fault lines" and "disagreements," as Faigley points out, "over the subjectivities that teachers of [creative] writing want students to occupy?"

Goldsmith's failure with "The Body of Michael Brown" isn't merely a matter of bad decision-making—to reappropriate the literal body of Michael Brown and to use his reappropriation for aesthetic ends. Rather, Goldsmith's failure was not recognizing the limits of his own poetics, not understanding the subject position from which he read and the ideology such subjectivity actively shaped. It strikes me as odd that the person who wrote an academic monograph about the poetics and theoretical framing of his own work—*Uncreative Writing*—doesn't think that briefly contextualizing one's work at a reading is within the scope of an artist's responsibility. But ultimately, that's beside the point, which is this: Goldsmith's technologically mediated poetics led him to occupy a subject position of alarming sociopolitical status. He adopted the voice of the State—the autopsy report—without explanation and then, accordingly, drew from his audience the criticism of the state. While we can, as Goldsmith shows us, speak through several voices not our own, creative writing studies, as it begins examining the ideological spaces its classrooms ask student writers to occupy, as Morton and Zavarzadeh would have us do, must begin the project of framing ways to investigate what it means to occupy multiple voices or voices not our own across digital landscapes occupied by the creative writer.

Landscape as canvas: Rhythm science

In *Fragments of Rationality*, Faigley reminds us that the ways in which subjectivity has been imagined in composition studies tend to privilege the (re)production of stable, rational, modernist selves and that the pursuit of "authentic" voice, fraught with the possibility of constructing "false consciousness," inevitably calls into question the ways in which composition classrooms position student writers in relation to their writing. He also examines the claims surrounding subjectivity that expressivist arguments for the teaching of writing have advocated, especially in terms of what such arguments present as the qualities of "good writing." Terms like "honest," for example, and "interesting" and even "authentic" are problematic for Faigley because they are so slippery and ultimately vague (113). Citing Catherine Belsey's *Critical Practice*, Fiagley claims that "two metaphors for language . . . have been dominant during the nineteenth and twentieth centuries: one the empiricist metaphor of language as the transparent window on reality, the other the expressivist metaphor of language as the vehicle for projecting the thoughts and emotions of the individual" (112). He points out that Belsey's merging of the two metaphors, "expressive realism," "resolves some of the major tensions within modernism by fusing realism and romanticism" (112). That fusing, in terms of creative writing studies and its capacity to produce artists with self-conscious subjectivity, is worth quoting at length here:

> Realism assumes that language can transmit directly what is signified in external reality. With the romantics came the belief that emotions could be transmitted directly as well; hence literature and art became both mimetic and expressive. The task of the author, poet, or artist was seen as twofold: the artist must represent reality accurately and convey to the viewer the heightened emotions that the artist has experienced. This theory treats the experience of reading as unproblematic. The universal "truths" contained in great art and literature are available to anyone with adequate facilities to discern them. That readers may be from different cultures, different classes, and of different genders does not matter because reading is perceived as the one-way flow from one autonomous mind to another, and the text is a self-contained object for passive consumption. While the implications of expressive realism for the reading of literature were widely studied in the 1980s, the consequences for the teaching of writing have only begun to be investigated. (112)

Investigating those consequences on the teaching of writing has required examining the ways in which digital environments put a variety of reading/ writing practices, as well as traditions, texts, and technotexts, into contact with each other. In his book, *Rhythm Science*, a popular and often cited argument in digital composition, Paul Miller explains this in terms of a "multiplex consciousness" that develops in those spaces. Citing W. E. B. Du Bois' notion of "double consciousness," Miller identifies a way of framing twenty-first century web-culture consciousness through a lineage that also include Charles-Mingus, who developed a third consciousness, one who watched the other two, unconcerned and unmoved. Miller claims that "where Du Bois saw duality and Mingus imagined a trinity, I would say that the twenty-first century self is so fully immersed in and defined by the data that surrounds it, we are entering an era of multiplex consciousness" (61).

Miller's book is itself as engaged with digitality as Monson's, or Hayles's, or Goldsmith's. His book, highlighting the multimodal ways in which digital environments have impacted art, is as visual as it is textual and as aural as it is visual. Its graphic design is an integral part of his argument and the book comes with a CD that works as an aural representation and extension of his argument: that web culture and digital tools have worked toward such a rapid reframing of what it means to produce art in the twenty-first century that new ways—inherently multimodal and interdisciplinary, perhaps even nondisciplinary—of imagining the act of composition—written or musical— must be constructed. The role of writing in such spaces is an invaluable way of weaving those modes together:

> There's something about the labor of writing and the sense of being part of the continuum of writing that goes back thousands of years. It is an ancient form, and in some ways it doesn't quite fit what's happening. The challenge then is to describe or characterize what it feels like to be alive now in the midst of it, but using this other mode of communication. . . . There's a reflexivity that comes with having to compose and letting language come through you. It's a different speed, there's slowness there. And I'm attracted to writing's infectiousness, the way you pick up language from other writers and remake it as your own. This stance is not contradictory: DJing is writing, writing is DJing. (56)

For Goldsmith, making other writers' voices his own, an act of appropriation that he sees as uniquely required of the creative writer in the digital age, is an act of literal repurposing. In contrast, Miller sees it as an act of mixing, one that the metaphor of the DJ allows him to explain. In fact, just like Hayles, Miller adopts a cipher, what he calls a "fiction" in order to do so, DJ Spooky (That Subliminal Kid), who is, he goes on to explain

> a living engagement with an ultra media-saturated youth culture. Creating this identity allowed me to spin narratives on several fronts at the same time and to produce persona as shareware. I started DJ-ing as a conceptual art project, but as the Spooky persona took on a life of its own, I came to regard it as a social sculpture, coding a generative syntax for new languages of creativity. "Spooky" grew from the fact that the disembodied music I loved—hip-hop, techno, ambient, futurjazz, spacedub—was itself a syntactic space reflecting the world I knew. (13)

Miller constructs an avatar that he describes as "a social sculpture, coding a generative syntax for new languages of creativity." To engage in digital environments, in other words, requires acknowledging that not only is multimodality a rich site in which to examine the ways textuality and aurality refract through each other, but also that there are "generative" possibilities "for new languages of creativity." Rather than surrender to the "unoriginal," as Goldsmith does, Miller constructs a method for sustained creativity within the digital environments that have grown out of industrialized cultural production. Rhythm science grows out of not only a nostalgic sense of tradition, but also the ways in which multiple traditions collide and refract in cultural environments. What this means in terms of writing instruction or "expressive realism," or one way in which we see composition as answering Faigley's call to investigate what "expressive realism" means in the writing classroom and the subjectivities it contributes to, can be found in Jeff Rice's work. Specifically, in "The Making of Ka-Knowledge: Digital Aurality," Jeff Rice explains:

> In digital culture, the process of interweaving composition and identity, of becoming an extension of one's own writing, of assembling various genres of discourse, has come to be known not as the stitch, but the mix. "In the mix," DJ Spooky wrote, "creator and remixer are woven together in the syncretic space of the text of samples and other sonic material." In the mix, we generate ka-knowledge. (273)

Ka-knowledge, for Rice, resists the exclusivity of visually based rhetorics for the sake of examining how aurality contributes to our technologically situated rhetorics. Rice carves out a kind of knowledge that values new kinds of knowing processes, processes that disrupt the privileging of print culture—its linearity and syllogistic reasoning—in order to "map out a 'ka-knowledge' necessary for a digital writing whose logic stems from aurality" (268). Miller wants to show us a writing built out of and with multiple modes. Rice wants to show us a writing built out of listening, a writing produced by ka-knowledge that reproduces new processes of knowing.[3] In order to do so, he recognizes that we need to examine the limits of heuristic ways of knowing and move toward a knowledge designed from methods of production, rather than, for example, critical, consumptive methods.

Miller yields to multiplicities of traditions that inevitably interact (often in surprising ways) across "the electromagnetic canvas" of our digital environments. That realm, Miller suggests, is not at odds with a conception of art that seeks to awaken human needs and desires oppressed by political and institutional forces by virtue of the alternative configurations possible through using that realm as a canvas across which to write. In other words, a networked culture in which technologies of inscription ranging from print to software make possible a proliferation of cultural patterns, the creation of art from out of the flow of such proliferation can make possible a sustained examination of as well as participation in oppressed human needs and desires—the interanimation of the rhetorical and the creative. The DJ, seen here, is a rhetorician; the rhetorician is an artist. By sampling from multiple cultural contexts and modes, the DJ makes new ways of imagining those contexts possible, and in this way we can begin to make sense from out of the fractured, contingent, and often contradictory ways in which those contexts engage. In other words, the composition of art from out of the digital flow of a culture seems to be an act that requires simultaneous attention to the act of creation as well as the act of examination. In this way, the work of Miller and Rice helps us see more clearly a way for creativity to thrive in a web-based culture.[4]

Faigley claims that approaches to literacy that "perceive [texts] as a one way flow from one autonomous mind to another, and [in which] the text is a self-contained object for passive consumption" are disrupted in the wake of postmodern theory, which composition has had a difficult time approaching. However, the kind of digital literacy Rice imagines, one that sees flow as multidirectional and multimodal, approaches postmodern theory in a way that asks us to reframe the act of composition itself. "To enact or practice ka-knowledge as digital writing," Rice explains,

> our narrative of literacy acquisition can no longer be topos based. . . . ka-knowledge . . . is a mixing, a usage of a variety of ideas, events, moments, and texts for the mix and the subsequent identity of "being mixed," not for the demonstration of expertise (a fixed topos-bound concept). (276)

Indeed, such an unmooring is what makes ka-knowledge so valuable. "Ka-knowledge is the digital rhetorical practice of assemblage," Rice claims (277). By drawing from DJ Spooky, the Notorious B.I.G. and the Beastie Boys, Rice has himself constructed an assemblage in the form of a theory that allows us to approach digital literacy and writing in a way that doesn't ask such literacy and writing to be new uses of the old (visual, print) ways. The mix is as auditory as it is visual, and these have a stake in the ways in which we derive value from digital writing.

To summarize: Goldsmith's digital poetics and Miller's "mix" argue that new ways of creative writing emerge in digital culture and digital environments. For Goldsmith, this includes primarily acts of appropriation and an attendant "post-identity politics." For Miller, this includes primarily the interanimation of multiple modes (visual, aural, textual) and ways of being "creative" as well as an attendant "multiplex consciousness." The ways digital environments mediate creative writers, in other words, affect who they are—they present new and emerging reading/writing practices that shape the subjectivities at work in the creative writing classroom. Rice points out that subscribing to a subjectivity bound to literacy practices exclusive to what he calls topos-based perpetuates a kind of expertise-oriented subjectivity. The production of imaginative texts, as creative writing studies begins the work of "further inventing" itself along digital lines, is inevitably bound up in such considerations.

A lot has changed since the publication of Morton and Zavarzadeh's article. While particular ideological positions are staked out in print-based creative writing practices and pedagogy (positions that privilege the "transparency" of print as a technology) that perhaps go unremarked on, examining how creative writing imagines itself in digital environments inevitably requires retheorizing those ideological positions and taking into account the subjectivities they shape. In a digital environment, in the mix, we encounter an immersive experience with language, one that uses print, sound, image, video, song, etc. In the mix we find the fashioning of poetic knowledge alongside the fashioning of rhetorical knowledge. Goldsmith's poetics and Miller's mix show us a spectrum across which creative writing is reoriented in digital environments and, as a result, a spectrum of subjectivities to consider emerge: the thief and plunderer on one end and a multiplex consciousness on the other. Whether a writer is adopting an other's voice, adapting his or her's or an other's voice, or remixing any of this for particular effect in digital environments, the role such examinations play in a digital branch of creative writing studies will inevitably require investigating issues regarding a range of identity politics—ownership, the relationship between authenticity and artificiality, and the ethics of representation, just to name a few touched upon by the above examples. But for the sake of the argument of this book, I turn in the next section toward what this means for the academic creative writer at a time when the development of creative writing studies stands to reimagine the relationship between writer and institution.

Authors, institutions, and ideology

"Frankly," Paul Miller writes in *Rhythm Science*, "by the start of the twenty-first century, the academy is such a reflection of class structure and hierarchy that it tends to cloud any real progressive contexts of criticism and discourse. By DJing, making art, and writing simultaneously, I tried to bypass the notion of the critic as an authority who controls narrative, and to create a new role that's resonant with web culture: to function as content provider, producer, and critic all at the same time. It is role consolidation as digital performance" (48). Rice's argument for the writer in digital spaces follows a similar logic, one that rejects the topos-based ideological position of expertise that inevitably follows from monomodal-based models of literacy acquisition. Writing, along the lines established by Rice and Miller, requires less "controlling the narrative" than it does slipping into multiple narratives (whether they be textual, aural, or visual) and weaving new pieces out of them. Recruiting different voices, employing a variety of modes, and remixing our ideological position's reroutes what we would traditionally call an "author" as imagined as a stable, modernized self, deliberative, rational, and instrumental in her language use. One could argue that it reroutes her toward nonexpert status that conflicts with the kind of subject position university structures claim to create.

This puts writing once again at odds with the university structure. Recall that expressivists often found themselves at odds with the disciplinary voices they heard the university asking students to adopt. And as Goldsmith, Hayles, Miller, and Rice show us, the role of "the self" to any writer is necessarily complex, especially when writers traffic in the refraction that takes place in digital environments. As print and digital ideologies continue to inform the practices of creative writers, we see developments that carry significance across a variety of areas for the creative writer: the use of digital tools, the shaping effect of those tools on her work, and, most importantly to this chapter, the effect such opportunity has on the subjectivity at work there. It would seem, given the state of the spectrum of subjectivity available to the creative writing interested in developing a digital understanding of producing imaginative texts, that such interest would divert her away from expertise status—and toward a new kind of subjectivity, simultaneously shaped by print and digital ideological terrain that sometimes veers into and other times out of the academy, depending on what "counts" as scholarship.

In *Rhetoric and Reality*, James Berlin briefly historicizes creative writing's development in the academy alongside expressionistic rhetoric, which could be described as a proto-expressionism, pointing out that colleges tended to go through "predictable, evolutionary stages in arriving at creative writing courses. Schools first offered courses focusing on rhetorical principles, then combined rhetoric and composition, then offered composition alone, and, at last, developed distinctive creative writing courses" (80). Alongside new criticism, which was also developing in English departments at this time, Berlin points out that at this time and within this scheme "criticism and creativity are both ultimately based on intuition since all truth is finally the result of an original and private vision, or the original and private verification of an act of original and private vision" (81). This reinforces the idea of an individual and autonomous self that, as Berlin later points out in *Rhetorics, Poetics, and Cultures*, remains at work in conceptions of students and student writers well into the postmodern age, when a culture that actively denies to subjectivity the privileged rationalism of the Enlightenment self-rises to dominance around the university structure. Perhaps this is a major contribution to why creative writers feel simultaneously part of and rejected by the university structure: their work in and out of the academy largely asks them to be different kinds of writers.

Understanding creative writing as a technologically mediated act provides the emerging discipline with a way of framing how creative writing as a field stands to examine and produce subjectivities that require negotiating discursive environments that are bound up in both autonomous and "mixed" subjectivities produced in an era when, as Miller points out, our media-saturated culture offers new "generative codes" for creativity at the same time that it, as Berlin points out, produces university structures that reinforce the privileged rationalism of the Enlightenment self. Subjectivity in creative writing, then, can on one hand be easily described as contextualized within the genre a writer works: poetry, fiction, creative nonfiction. But as emerging technologies—specifically inscription technologies—make new kinds of writing and new ways of imagining writing available to the writer, creative writing stands poised to consider the writer as one who, to borrow from Miller, "functions as content provider, producer, and critic all at the same time."

Considering how these institutions (re)produce particular "selves," none of which we need to call "authentic," I consider in the next chapter the ways in which one mainstream author takes on the technological in a series of translated essays that, he argues, speak back to our technological moment in a powerful way, but one that, I will argue, reinforces the myth of the print and digital divide, one that is problematically perpetuated in our culture. As I hope this chapter made clear, that divide is more productively imagined as an ecology through which readers and writers live and work daily. In the chapters that follow, I will extend such logic to consider what such a creative writer can do with shifting understandings of genre and process, mobilized by an increasingly digitized culture, then, the chapter that follows, how this reorients our institutional practices in both creative writing and composition studies.

Notes

1 For more on the political history of creative writing programs, see Eric Bennet's *Workshops of Empire: Stegner, Engle, and American Creative Writing During the Cold War*, in which the development of the University of Iowa's creative writing program is examined alongside the political, ideological, and symbolic shifts of the Cold War.

2 In the next chapter, I will investigate those emerging forms on their own terms.

3 For more on music as a rhetorical trope, see Steven Katz's book *The Epistemic Music of Rhetoric: Toward the Temporal Dimension of Affect in Reader Response and Writing*, Thomas Rickert's article "Language's Duality and the Rhetorical Problem of Music," and Brian Vicker's article "Figure of Rhetoric/Figures of Music."

4 Postcritical, as I am using the term here, comes from the work of Greg Ulmer. For more material on the ways in which postcritical thought materializes in digital environments, see his book *Internet Invention: From Literacy to Electracy*.

4

Process, Genre, and Technologizing the Word

In the previous chapter, I argued that shifting definitions of authority within craft criticism expressly concerned with digital environments not only introduces us to ways of imagining the (multiple, often conflicting) subjectivities of the creative writer, especially in the classroom, but also requires that, as creative writing studies establishes itself within the academy, we attend to the complex ways in which writers are mediated according to twenty-first-century composing practices. Any framework for a digitally inflected understanding of creative writing inevitably requires that writers, in other words, pay close attention to the ways that digital environments shape what it means to be a writer, while accounting for a theoretical framework that helps us situate a writer's relationship to the ways in which new and emerging media are always negotiating the practice of producing an imaginative text.

In this chapter I extend this framework to include the ways in which genre—understood as the definable contours of a work even as it spills across, employs, or encounters a variety of media before its final draft—shifts within the development of new composing practices made available in digital environments. As Tim Mayers explains in "Creative Writing and Process Pedagogy," "One of the . . . things that seem[s] to have gone unnoticed for so long about the workshop (or at least not to have presented itself as a significant problem) [is] that the workshop as traditionally organized is a primarily product-oriented endeavor. . . . Creative writing as an activity is undoubtedly enmeshed with process. But workshop pedagogy often focuse[s] only on a single, frozen moment in that process; all of the real work (the 'process,' if you will) took place before and after that moment" (41). I am interested in melting that frozen moment. If the process of writing imaginative texts, in other words, can be opened up and examined across new and emerging media, then, of course, the products themselves—the genres—can change.

Much of the field of creative writing, furthermore, is organized through and by the genres of imaginative writing. It organizes course offerings (the poetry workshop, the fiction workshop). It stabilizes (or destabilizes) a writer's identity, as I address in the previous chapter. And it points us to the ways in which creative writing was and still is a product-oriented discipline. The "melting" of generic conventions across digital environments, then, reveals, to some degree, new paths for the field of creative writing studies to take, which I will examine in the next chapter. In this chapter, however, I work toward providing those paths according to the ways digital craft criticism encounters process and genre. To illustrate how generic conventions themselves begin to take into account the technological conditions within which they are situated, I turn toward writers from both within and outside of academia, but who all share an investment in the quality of our writing and reading lives in an increasingly new media-saturated cultural moment. Each of the authors I address in this chapter engages in craft criticism as it intersects with growing issues around technology and aesthetics. I will define their work not only as a digital kind of craft criticism, but a significant investigation into the ways digitized craft invites the technology to play a role in the contour of the work, which, I argue, helps scholars of creative writing studies develop sophisticated understandings of the ways genres blur and mature through electronic writing practices. At stake, as I will show, are the larger institutional structures within which creative writing studies imagines itself.

(Nervous) cultural conditions: Writing and the electromagnetic imaginary

Tim Mayers, in briefly examining the craft criticism of novelist Charles Baxter, points out that "the intersection between contemporary culture and the production of fiction" inevitably entails not only an "attempt to dismantle many operative assumptions about fiction writing, and in so doing challenge much of the institutional conventional wisdom about creative writing," but also the engagement between print practices and electronic ones:

> In his essay "Stillness," [Baxter] asks the provocative question, "What conceivable relation is there between narrative violence and data

processing?" (223) His answer, essentially, is that in a culture where information, especially through the medium of language, moves at an ever-increasing rate of speed, people find it easier to be "in touch" with violence than with stillness: "People who work all day at computers often get keyed up, tense, and anxious because of the speed of the information flow" (224). And this, he believes, has an inevitable effect on the way people are able to read (and, perhaps more important, to write) stories: "It's just possible that benign stillness has become a condition in our time that everyone feels now and then but which almost no one can describe with much accuracy. This has everything to do with what adult readers will believe and accept about their own past experiences. My sense of these matters is that we have become remarkably fluent in our narratives in describing violence and complaint but timid and insecure in describing moments of repose. In the nineteenth century, the reverse was true." (231)

Our cultural swapping of moments of repose for moments of violence, his argument implies, is the result of getting "keyed up" in front of the computer all day. Stillness is not a quality that he prescribes to computing culture. He argues that our hyper-connected and information-soaked age has led not only to negative connotations regarding what it means to be still—it is associated with "madness, mooncalfing, woolgathering, laziness, hostility, and stupidity"—but also to what he calls "information sickness." As Beverly Payano points out in a 2009 interview with Baxter in *The Rumpus*, according to Baxter's argument "it's the writer's job to transform information at the data level into a story with which readers can experience and relate. The constant bombardment of information, however, threatens the writer's ability to transform data into fiction, thus trapping the reader at the data level as well." Later in the interview, Baxter explains: "Good fiction doesn't just convey information; it conveys—imparts—an experience. Meditation might help as a path to a reacquaintance with silence. But nothing works so well as a judicious shutting-down of screen culture: computer screens particularly."

Jonathan Franzen makes a similar move in his book *The Kraus Project*, in which he translates two of Austrian satirist Karl Kraus's early twentieth-century essays about poet Heinrich Heine and playwright Johann Nestroy. Franzen's book contains footnotes that not only supplement his translations, but become an undercurrent within the book itself (almost, one wants to say, like hypertext) through which another subterranean narrative unfolds, one that links Kraus's extensive criticism of technological innovations of his time (telephone, telegraph, high-speed printing press) with Franzen's extensive criticism of the technological innovations of his time (social media, blogs, high-speed online journalism). Nested within these connections is also a narrative that describes Franzen's time as a Fulbright scholar abroad reading Kraus and his eventual intellectual awakening. Franzen weaves himself into Kraus's essays both argumentatively and personally and argues that

> Kraus has more to say to us in our own media-saturated, technology-crazed, apocalypse-haunted historical moment than his more accessible contemporaries do now. He himself was well aware of the paradox: he was a farseeing prophet whose work was always focused on what was right in front of him. He was, very consciously, speaking to us.

Franzen in many ways extends Baxter's line of thinking regarding the cultural conditions surrounding writing. In unpacking Kraus's observation that the turn-of-century Germany allowed for the inappropriate influence of outside countries (particularly Italy and France) to shape its own cultural understanding of itself, Franzen makes an analogous connection on which he rests his argument as he sets it up above. That analogy makes synonymous the conditions surrounding artistic production in Germany before the First World War and the technology industry's influence on the economic and cultural landscape in the United States at the start of the twenty-first century. In short, Franzen reinforces the importance of cultural conditions that freeze genre into static conventions by working against an understanding of technology that renders cultural production a nostalgic or moot act. This doesn't mean that a novel can't carry significant social value (though Franzen has also published on the nervous conditions surrounding that), but rather that a very specific kind of novel is the best way for conveying significant social value—and technological innovation has only served its trivialization. For Franzen, as for Kraus and Baxter, rapidly changing technologies that surround the production of art are hazardous to that very process because they don't provide the right kind of conditions for producing such work. Franzen writes:

> [Kraus's argument] was aimed at bright and well-educated cultural authorities who embraced a phony kind of individuality—people Kraus believed should have known better. It's not clear that Kraus's shrill, ex

cathedra denunciations were the most effective way to change hearts and minds. But I confess to feeling some version of his disappointment when a novelist who I believe ought to have known better, Salman Rushdie, succumbs to Twitter. Or when a politically committed print magazine that I respect, *n+1*, denigrates print magazines as terminally "male," celebrates the internet as "female," and somehow neglects to consider the Internet's accelerating pauperization of freelance writers. Or when good lefty professors who once resisted alienation—who criticized capitalism for its restless assault on every tradition and every community that gets in its way—start calling the corporatized Internet "revolutionary," happily embrace Apple computers, and persist in gushing about their virtues. (12)

According to additional notes provided by scholar Paul Reitter, Heine "attempted to act as a cultural mediator. What he was hoping for—and going for, too—was a synthesis of opposites: of the life-affirming 'sensualism' he associated with the French and the intellectually rigorous culture of German 'spiritualism.'" (16). Franzen, then, serves much the same role here, and in fact goes so far as to say that the style in which Kraus wrote was so dense that it necessarily requires explanation alongside translation and Franzen, as translator, is, in this regard, our guide, our mediator. His argument props up an understanding of culture as suffering apocalyptically from a synthesis of opposites: an understanding of technology that is insufferably linked with being "cool"—his opening metaphor is the old Apple computer advertising campaign of Mac versus PC, in which the actor portraying the Mac was, according to Franzen, smug, and, according to the culture, "cool"—and an understanding of art that doesn't participate in the automatic validation of cultural denigration committed in the name of "innovation." Technology, along these lines, is something that seduces us and distracts us from more rigorous and important work. Franzen's extrapolation of Kraus's argument into our own culture (and cultural moment) works as a mediation and act of cultural preservation, one that aims to slow down the "progress" made in the name of technological "innovation" because it is ultimately at the cost of a more valuable understanding and practice of art.

At stake for Kraus and Franzen is the trivialization of culture and the diverse ways that emerging media find in order to continually perpetuate its trivialization.

For Baxter the problem is a matter of the cultural conditions of information acceleration and its effects on our culture's capacity to register "stillness." For Franzen, those same cultural conditions amount to a culture so intoxicated with technological advancements that it can no longer participate responsibly in the often difficult but rewarding work of countercultural exploration that art is supposed to serve. Franzen's argument also resonates with arguments that float through the publishing industry and its perennial "death" in the age of electronic reading and Amazon sales. How can we, so the argument goes, contribute to the difficult yet rewarding process of examining cultural and social conditions—of which art and imaginative writing are supposed to be a vital part—when the very landscape of those conditions is shifting so rapidly?

Creative writing as an academic discipline is in a unique position to consider such a question. Franzen and Baxter, in short, as craft critics, essentially argue that the cultural conditions surrounding creative production are increasingly ominous and we are losing allies to the seductive and problematic posture such ominousness takes in our lives. The implication here is that these conditions threaten to change how we read and write imaginative texts:

> Around 1908 [Kraus] came to believe that our technological capabilities and our imaginative faculties were going in opposite directions—the former were going up and, as a result, the latter down—and this thought really scared him. . . . To me the most impressive thing about Kraus as a thinker may be how early and clearly he recognized the divergence of technological progress from moral and spiritual progress. A succeeding century of the former, involving scientific advances that would have seemed miraculous not long ago, has resulted in high-resolution smartphone videos of dudes dropping Mentos into liter bottles of Diet Pepsi and shouting "Whoa!" while they geyser. Techno-visionaries of the 1990s promised that the Internet would usher in a new world of peace, love, and understanding, and Twitter executives are still banging the utopianist drum, claiming foundational credit for the Arab Spring. To listen to them, you'd think it was inconceivable that Eastern Europe could liberate itself from the Soviets without the benefit of cell phones, or that a bunch of Americans revolted against the British and produced the U.S. Constitution without 4G capability. (140)

Since technology has given rise to shallow forms of entertainment (and, Franzen would add, problematic kinds of journalism) and is always bound up in sociopolitical conditions that continually validate it rather than provide substantive critiques of it, our imaginative processes are denigrated. The cause and effect of the conditions that he describes here—the technological capabilities that cause the denigration of our imaginative capabilities (after all, Eastern European liberation and American revolution happened alongside the technologies of their time—so maybe technology isn't the problem here)—are somewhat vague, but the cultural conditions within which imaginative writing takes place are not. As our culture increasingly embraces emerging technologies and the shady promises they make, our writers face an increasingly heightened challenge: to say something within and about the shifting plate tectonics of that culture *as they shift*.

Such an argument adheres to a definition of a mobile artist who maneuvers within the nostalgia for a fixed society. "As an artist," Franzen explains, "you want to be able to move liberally and sympathetically among various classes and cultures—just like Shakespeare did—*while secretly hoping that everyone who's not an artist will stay fixed in place. . . .* It's part of the dubious moral character that artists are famed for. And it helps make sense of how furiously Kraus rejected political categories. He wasn't just resisting the linguistically debased sloganeering of politics. He was insisting on the artist's uniquely privileged place in society. He argued for maintaining differences because he knew his kind of art—maybe all good art—depends on it" (159, original emphasis).

When that society and culture begins to shift, as emerging technologies increasingly make possible, then the very definition of an artist is at stake. Indeed, it seems almost to collapse. The counter argument, of course, is that they proliferate. The effect of such an approach within Franzen's argument, as a result, ultimately works toward calcifying what we mean by literature or imaginative writing. Franzen and Baxter require the contours surrounding their art of choice—the novel—to remain strong and steadfastly faithful to what we expect a novel to look like. The experience that Baxter wants to preserve (through the shutting of computer screens) and that Franzen wants to protect (by policing the ways in which emerging technologies distract us from more important political, cultural, and aesthetic ways of being) necessarily requires that we do not allow technology to affect what we talk about when we talk about (the writing of) literature.

But such arguments lack attention to how language as a technology itself arranges a particular kind of engagement with the world in the first place—and how, once such considerations are made, various other kinds of mediation can make the same kind of engagement possible. Obviously problems emerge when we consider that society is in flux—when we acknowledge the emergence of new media and their effect on the conditions of artistic production; one easy way to solve this problem is to cling to a (myth of) monomodal art and our inherited genres. But for artists who have worked toward aesthetic expression in an increasingly multimodal cultural landscape, such adherence to traditional forms ignores a central point: culture has always been multimodal; writers have always been navigating it. Franzen and Baxter combat it. As I discuss in Chapter 2, the work of Kenneth Goldsmith and Kodwu Eshun, among others, has pointed artists toward a lineage and direction in a cultural landscape increasingly producing new mediums. The technoculture that Franzen fears becomes, for these artists, the very fabric of expression. Recall that Paul Miller, in his alter-ego DJ Spooky, constructs an avatar that he describes as "a social sculpture, coding a generative syntax for new languages of creativity." To engage in digital environments, including their critique, in Miller's book *Rhythm Science*, requires acknowledging that not only is multimodality a rich site in which to examine the ways text, image, and sound refract through each other, but also that there are "generative" possibilities "for new languages of creativity" that can produce the kind of aesthetic experience that Franzen and Baxter both argue for. Rather than surrender to the machinations that, for Baxter or Franzen, distract or wash out truth in art, these artists construct a method for sustained creativity within the digital environments that have grown out of industrialized cultural production. What Miller calls "rhythm science"—a kind of art constructed out of music, textuality, images, and philosophy—grows out of not only the nostalgic sense of tradition as Franzen conceives of it, but also the ways in which multiple traditions collide and refract in digital cultural environments.

Miller's argument contrasts Franzen's (and Baxter's) by virtue of the way he imagines the resources available to the artist in an age of emerging technology. As I point out in Chapter 2, Kenneth Goldsmith in *Uncreative Writing*, challenges the way creative writing perpetuates a static (and undertheorized) understanding of writing, one enabled by the kind of understanding of technology that

Franzen and Baxter provide, one that also perpetuates an understanding of imaginative writing as confined to poetry, fiction, and creative nonfiction, three genres which dominate the field and whose dominance are reproduced in the textbook industry's implied insistence that these are the only forms that creative writing need concern itself with. Authors like Ander Monson, Mark Z Danielewski, and Jonathan Lethem, as well as those mentioned above work within an aesthetic paradigm in keeping with Miller's philosophy and, as a result, stand unaccounted for in arguments that seek to engage the role technology plays in the cultural conditions surrounding imaginative writing.

What does any of this have to do with genre? I contend that the arguments that work toward the calcification of genre and the print conditions from which it emerged require a retheorizing of how we account for genre within the field of creative writing as it approaches its digital turn. Arguments like Baxter's and Franzen's—arguments that freeze genre into its recognizable and inherited conventions and steep it firmly within a print tradition—concede to recognizing technology as, at best, a tool, something perhaps present at the scene of writing, but ultimately unimportant in the construction of an imaginative text. Using the work of Walter Ong and Martin Heidegger, I will examine in the next section the arguments of such craft criticism, then explore examples of digital craft criticism that examine genre and the conditions surrounding genre that point to, as I will show, a reorientation of the field of creative writing as it has been historically situated according to print-oriented understandings of poetry, fiction, and creative nonfiction. I will continue such an examination into the next chapter more explicitly in terms of the wider possibilities that such a reorientation makes possible for the institutional practices of creative writing.

Writing as technology

As has been widely observed in composition studies, the study of literacy in relation to orality has yielded a productive understanding of writing as a technology that externalizes, organizes, and mediates thought. In his influential article, "Writing is a Technology that Restructures Thought," Walter Ong outlines the historical and theoretical turns that undergird the historical paradigm shift of moving from orality to literacy (which begins in antiquity but still exists in various stages in cultures today), arguing that not only is writing a technology that hyper-literate humans have internalized to the point of no longer considering it a technology, but that when we acknowledge that it is a technology—it is an artificial system and interface through which we apply and engage our will for desired outcomes—invaluable findings can be made regarding the function of literacy in hyper-literate cultures. "We can now," he explains, " view in better perspective the world of writing in which we live, see better what this world really is, and what functionally literate human beings really are—that is, beings whose thought processes do not grow out of simply natural powers but out of these powers as structured, directly or indirectly, by the technology of writing. Without writing, the literate mind would not and could not think as it does, not only when engaged in writing but even when it is composing its thoughts in oral form."

Simply put, writing is perhaps our most intimate technology—and one whose status as technology has historically receded from our attention. Ong goes on to explain that once understood this way, writing and computers can be seen to share historical arguments against them:

> Writing was an intrusion, though an invaluable intrusion, into the early human lifeworld, much as computers are today. It has lately become fashionable in some linguistic circles to refer to Plato's condemnation of writing in the *Phaedrus* and the Seventh Letter. What is seldom if ever noticed, however, is that Plato's objections against writing are essentially the very same objections commonly urged today against computers by those who object to them (Ong 1982: 79–81). Writing, Plato has Socrates say in the *Phaedrus*, is inhuman, pretending to establish outside the mind what in reality can only be in the mind. Writing is simply a thing, something to be manipulated, something inhuman, artificial, a manufactured product. We recognize here the same complaint that is made against computers: they are artificial contrivances, foreign to human life.

The development of writing, something Plato cautions us against as it would cripple our memories, dehumanize communication (it takes the spoken away from the speaker), and cannot be grounded or (therefore) trusted, inevitably leads us to reconsider Franzen's and Baxter's arguments, not necessarily to prove them wrong or to laud all things technological because writing is among them, but rather to reframe writing given these considerations and adapt those arguments in order to explore and examine what imaginative writing looks like when it is understood to be a technology that engages with other emerging technologies in an increasingly media-saturated culture. As Ong explains:

> One weakness in Plato's position is that he put these misgivings about writing into writing, just as one weakness in anti-print positions is that their proponents put their objections into print, and one weakness in anti-computer positions is that they are articulated in articles or books printed from tapes composed on computer terminals. The law at work here is: once the word is technologized, there is no really effective way to criticize its condition without the aid of the technology you are criticizing. The complaints about these three inventions are all the same because writing and print and the computer are all ways of technologizing the word.

To reconsider Baxter's and Franzen's arguments in light of such an understanding of technology is to admit that it exists in what Paul Miller calls "the mix," the cultural landscape as it provides emerging canvases—and becomes a canvas itself—across which artists—writers included—can work. Then we can examine genre (as it is itself a form of technology) in a new and more productive light.

Before framing Baxter's and Franzen's arguments this way, however, it will help to clear up some relationships among art, technology, artist, and culture. In his essay "The Question Concerning Technology," Martin Heidegger works toward such ends by pursuing a definition of what he calls the "essence" of technology. In line with Franzen's thinking, Heidegger points out that as long as we merely adopt and perpetuate the technological, we will always be under its control: "We shall never experience our relationship to the essence of technology so long as we merely conceive and push forward the technological, put up with it, or evade it. Everywhere we remain unfree and chained to technology, whether we passionately affirm or deny it" (287). To understand the "essence" of technology is to liberate ourselves through an understanding of how it functions in our lives, including the ways in which it, in making our lives functional, recedes from our attention. In order to do this, Heidegger defines technology according to two prongs: (1) it is "a means to an end," or a tool; and (2) it is a "human activity." We participate with it even if we evade its role in our lives. Questioning technology according to these definitions, then, provides Heidegger with a path for exposing its essence—how it manipulates and shapes meaning in our lives—something that Heidegger insists is not in itself a technological endeavor (it is philosophical), and, as a result, his line of questioning works toward an understanding of technology that, to use Ong's words, accounts for how it "structures, directly or indirectly," our own being and ways of knowing that being.

Technology, then, becomes ontological and epistemological. It is intimately bound up with how we know what we know about the world. (Indeed, never has this been more true than it has been in "the information age," as Baxter laments.) As Graham Harman puts it in *Tool-Being: Heidegger and the Metaphysics of Objects*: "Heidegger might claim that even if technology doesn't really denude the world of all its mysteries, it is a danger insofar as it makes us *think* that it does so, makes us *believe* that the cosmos has been adequately revealed as a stockpile" (188). Technology's presence in our lives makes particular ways of being and knowing possible. Therefore, Heidegger warns, we must be vigilant in our understanding of how it works. He claims that technology "enframes" our being; it is a way of ordering the world and we must bring forth ways of understanding it as such (as a poet, in Heidegger's understanding of a poet, does, but more on that later). Because we come to rely on it so much, we lose sight of how technology turns around and manipulates us, turns humans into what he calls "standing-reserves." The example Heidegger uses to illustrate this is a forester who works at the command of the paper industry:

> The forester who, in the wood, measures the felled timber and to all appearances walks the same forest path in the same way as did his grandfather is today commanded by profit-making in the lumber industry, whether he knows it or not. He is made subordinate to the orderability of cellulose, which for its part is challenged forth by the need for paper, which is then delivered to newspapers and illustrated magazines. The latter, in their turn, set public opinion to swallowing what is printed, so that a set configuration of opinion becomes available on demand. Yet precisely because man is challenged more originally than are the energies of nature, i.e., into the process of ordering, he never is transformed into mere standing-reserve. Since man drives technology forward, he takes part in ordering as a way of revealing. But the unconcealment itself, within which ordering unfolds, is never a human handiwork, any more than is the realm through which man is already passing every time he as a subject relates to an object.

Technology's power isn't so much in what it can do for us, or in what we can make it do, but rather in how it matters as an experience within which we participate. Such an experience shapes our way of thinking and being and Heidegger's philosophy asks us to see the essence of technology, which is revealed as not in itself technological, and open up new ways of being that are not limited by, enframed within, or at the mercy of technology's presence in our lives.

Understood this way, we see ourselves surrounded by technologies. Emerging media are a part of a larger set of relations we have with the world. What's more is that we can see that *writing* has receded from our attention as a technology and creative writing's standing-reserves—the genres we practice: fiction, poetry, creative nonfiction—come to define our experiences with that technology to a degree that, I would contend, makes it difficult to see other ways of being or knowing. Poets, for Heidegger, make the conditions through which meaning emerges visible—poetry changes how we know by revealing the essence of these conditions and showing us a new way of thinking about them. The technology of writing, which Ong makes visible for us, and which Heidegger makes ontological for us, becomes, as we can see in Franzen's argument, that which has receded in its naturalization and so, therefore, other uses are foreclosed. Put another way: writing, in Franzen's argument, is a way to combat emerging technologies and the havoc they bring to our culture (and mental processes). For the novelist, this means adhering to the naturalized state of such writing and remaining unconcerned with its own status as a technology. Ong and Heidegger point us toward another way of imagining the production of such combat, one that situates writing as one among a constellation of other media and the ontological effect of acknowledging such constellations.

The effect on our understanding of genre is wide-ranging. As Mayers puts it, "Heidegger's thinking . . . allows both creative writers and compositionists to confront and challenge the horribly limiting and counterproductive definitions of writing that have held sway both inside and outside of the academy for so long" (95). As Franzen's argument illustrates, a definition of writing that puts it at odds with technology not only limits what we allow writers and artists to do in a culture that is increasingly introducing new media, but perhaps more importantly, limits *how* they are able to do it. The contours we draw around artistic production, *and the more we reinforce them as the default conditions that define the field,* in other words, threaten to conceal artistic production in a paradigm that refuses to take into account the technological conditions of artistic production. For Franzen, writers exist at the margins of a technological society that increasingly trivializes poetic and novelistic writing while refusing to acknowledge the ways in which writers challenge that society. For Ong, writing is one of those technologies, and for Heidegger, the writer—the poet— has a responsibility to remember that and to use poetic meaning (a kind of meaning I consider inherent in all imaginative writing) as a way to see past the ready-made or standing-reserve world presented to us and to reveal the essence of that world.

In creative writing (perhaps more than any other field) that ready-made world is reinforced through genre. As Mark McGurl makes clear in *The Program Era: Postwar Fiction and the Rise of Creative Writing,* Wilbur Schramm's *The Story Workshop* (1938), Caroline Gordon and Allen Tate's *The House of Fiction* (1950), Cleanth Brooks and Robert Penn Warren's *Understanding Fiction* (1943/1959), and, I would add John Gardner's *The Art of Fiction* and Madison Smartt Bell's *Narrative Design* circulated near-canonically throughout creative writing programs in higher education in the twentieth century. For McGurl it's important to notice that these textbook-anthologies pointed creative writing students toward a narrow understanding of *discipline*: "discipline meant obedience to rules, and rules were established and maintained by institutions [who adopted these textbook-anthologies]" (McGurl 135). The result, for McGurl's argument, is the homogenizing effect of textbook-anthologies (and workshop pedagogy) on the emerging discipline of creative writing. For our purposes here, it's important to point out that the textbook-anthology in creative writing programs creates ready-mades and standing-reserves in the shape of what we can call literary fiction. Such a process calcifies genre. Several scholars have cited the effect these ready-mades have had on the production of literature in postwar America (*Talents and Technicians, The Program Era*) and I refer to them here not to argue against their presence or to admonish them, but simply in order to identify the ways in which these genres have become technologies themselves, albeit intimate technologies with rich traditions, but technologies that nevertheless dovetail now with emerging ones. That interaction asks us to reconsider how we define those genres in light of the conditions that reproduce as well as alter them. In other words, the creative writer in many ways has become the forester at the mercy of the paper industry. Heidegger's example works here as a rich metaphor: the creative writer risks becoming a standing-reserve when the technology around him, in which he is always implicated, only makes one relationship available. Put another way: What else could that creative writer be doing in the woods? Must he be reproducing that which technology—in this case the technology of genre (the industrialized and technologized word)—requires him to? Isn't there more exploring to be done? Must Franzen echo Kraus? Or are there new ways of saying what he means? I'm not, in other words, claiming that Franzen's argument is wrong. I'm saying it needs to consider itself within the media ecology that produced it—literary writing. When examined as a technology itself, then we can see that the sort of countercultural criticism he aims for in his footnotes to Kraus's book—footnotes that reinforce print-oriented contours of what it means to write—then we begin to allow for other ways of Franzen's argument to find articulation.

In *Rhythm Science,* Miller argues that "there's something about the labor of writing and the sense of being part of the continuum of writing that goes back thousands of years. It is an ancient form, and in some ways it doesn't quite fit what's happening." He goes on to explain that "the challenge then is to describe or characterize what it feels like to be alive now in the midst of it, but using this other mode of communication . . . . There's a reflexivity that comes with having to compose and letting language come through you. It's a different speed, there's slowness there. And I'm attracted to writing's infectiousness, the way you pick up language from other writers and remake it as your own. This stance is not contradictory: DJing is writing, writing is DJing" (56). Miller is useful again here because we hear him using the same language as Baxter, Franzen, Ong, and Heidegger. Miller refers to the "slowness" of writing, the "ultra media-saturated youth culture" it increasingly encounters, the "generative syntax" and "new languages of creativity" he works toward producing within the social sculpture and conceptual art project he calls DJ Spooky. (Seen in this way, Franzen could be understood as a remixed version of Kraus.) Miller's book is as aural as it is textual, as visual as it is literary. The ways these modes refract through each other work toward an understanding of what it means for creative production to encounter the conditions of the emerging media it uses in order to, as Miller puts it, "describe or characterize what it feels like to be alive now in the midst of it." If Franzen has a problem with industrialized technology, then he should also have a problem with industrialized writing (the literary novel, the ways genres are used on the marketplace in order to shape particular ways of knowing). What does the acknowledgment of writing as one medium circulating through a media ecology in an increasingly digital cultural landscape allow us to see regarding genre? How does it fit into a larger understanding of what it means to further understand the relationship between composition studies and creative writing?

Miller as a digital craft critic points out that Baxter's and Franzen's arguments aren't wrong, but limited. The stillness that Baxter desires and the generative syntax (or imagination) that Franzen claims is lost are both, in Miller's argument, working toward a method that asks artists to participate in the construction of new genres that interact with the new technologies from which they emerge, including writing (and print traditions). As I point out in Chapter 2, books like Ander Monson's *Vanishing Point*, stories like Jennifer Egan's "Black Box" and Rick Moody's "Some Contemporary Characters," both published through Twitter, demonstrate that "succumbing" to Twitter, as Franzen puts it, does not require painting all textual production on Twitter with the same brush. Miller, in using multiple modes, reveals writing as a technology—the oldest, with a "continuum . . . that goes back thousands of years." Working with/in multiple technologies frees Miller to see "creativity" in a new way. He embodies Heidegger's "essence" of technology insofar as he is interested in producing new relationships with it that reveal "generative syntaxes." Should we, then, continue studying and practicing writing on its own terms because of its history and status as our most intimate technology? Sure. But should we also develop new ways of imagining how it comes into contact with other modes? Can we expand the field in order to account for how and why writers do that? Of course.

By virtue of their engagement with the emerging technologies with which they come into contact, hybridized genres are difficult to pin down. Egan's reader on *The New Yorker's* Twitter page writes that Egan is actually writing narrative poetry. Moody claims that writing through Twitter's platform felt more like writing haiku. Miller calls these canvases "the mix." In Moody and

Egan's cases, writers and readers recruited other genres to help understand the modifications of the genre that surfaced through the interaction of stories and the platform those stories were published through. As Marshal McLuhan argued in *Understanding Media*, any cool medium is going to require the participation of its audience to fully express the potential of that medium—and as we use the vocabulary of (and ideological baggage associated with) print-based understandings of genre to understand how they blur and evolve in digital spaces—the *genre* category of a digital craft criticism points us toward how generic conventions are resisted (as they are in *Vanishing Point: Not a Memoir*) or mutated (as they are in the "live" stories of the tweeted work of Rick Moody and Jennifer Egan). In short, identifying and investigating the ways digitized notions of craft invite the technology to play a role in the contour of the work helps scholars of creative writing studies develop sophisticated understandings of the ways genres blur and mature through electronic writing practices.

It should come as no surprise, of course, that the web has a strong and healthy population of not just online creative writing journals, but also websites devoted to the various mutations electronic environments make possible. While a catalogue of such journals and sites is beyond the scope of this chapter, it's important to note that they create a site within which notions of craft are regularly fashioned and refashioned and through which print and digital understandings of genre continually shape each other, creating an arena within which craft stands to be discussed in self-reflective ways. I want to extend this line of thinking to argue that such considerations are, in effect, considerations of process. To examine digital craft criticism regarding genre requires, to a large degree, the examination of process as well. If form follows meaning as it refracts through emerging technologies and increasingly invites new ways of shaping genre, then how does the field of creative writing studies begin to account for a theory of genre that affords a writer such fluidity? What are the repercussions on how the field operates and identifies itself? In other words, I hope that I have demonstrated the complex ways in which genre is shaped by an emerging digital craft criticism—in order to now examine how such complexity asks us to reorient genre and process within creative writing studies so as to approach a wider understanding of how that field stands to contribute to the production of knowledge.

Genre, process, and the production of knowledge

Genre in digital craft criticism necessarily requires that we consider how print-oriented genres are (re)produced in the field of creative writing studies and how *at the same time* emerging media alert us to genre's status as a ready-made and the potential to craft new hybrid forms with new emerging media. As we have seen in earlier chapters, writers like Kenneth Goldsmith and Ander Monson reframe the poetic concept to consider genre as a flexible set of conditions. Reading from traffic reports at the White House *as poetry* presents new ways of thinking about everyday life and "gridlocked" politics. Weaving his personal narrative and cultural criticism between his book and the internet allows Monson to craft what he calls "not a memoir," insofar as its form often requires his book to veer away from himself and becomes a text that exists somewhere in-between our current categorical systems. Such texts are made possible by practices informed by digital tools and environments. Genre, as it is employed in digital environments, is itself a kind of process. A process of developing new kinds of texts and new kinds of meaning with new kinds of media.

The course description for Kenneth Goldsmith's Uncreative Writing class at the University of Pennsylvania reads:

> It's clear that long-cherished notions of creativity are under attack, eroded by file-sharing, media culture, widespread sampling, and digital replication. How does writing respond to this new environment? This workshop will rise to that challenge by employing strategies of appropriation, replication, plagiarism, piracy, sampling, plundering, as compositional methods. Along the way, we'll trace the rich history of forgery, frauds, hoaxes, avatars, and impersonations spanning the arts, with a particular emphasis on how they employ language. We'll see how the modernist notions of chance, procedure, repetition, and the aesthetics of boredom dovetail with popular culture to usurp conventional notions of time, place, and identity, as all expressed linguistically. (201)

I point this out here to demonstrate that this is a course description for a creative writing course not defined by the genres it aims to reproduce, but rather the "strategies" it aims to employ. In describing the way(s) his students respond to and work within the course, he explains "that they were much more oriented to consuming online culture than seeing it as something to create new works from. Although we were engaging in a meaningful two-way conversation, I felt there was a real pedagogical need to be filled, one that centered around issues of contextualization. And there were big gaps of knowledge. It was as if all the pieces were there, but they needed someone to help put them together in the right place and in the right order, a situation that called for a conceptual reorientation of what already came naturally to them" (202). The projects students commit to in such a course are demonstrative of one way in which creative writing stands to produce knowledge regarding writing practices and traditions, as opposed to reproducing genres in the classroom. Goldsmith, in framing his course through strategies and conceptual reorientation, sets up a way in which to imagine how creative writing studies as an academic discipline, can contribute to meaningful discussions about what it means to produce imaginative texts in digital environments.

Bronwyn T. Williams, in his essay "Digital Technologies and Creative Writing Pedagogy," examines "how concepts that digital media allow intersect with concepts particularly relevant to creative writing pedagogy" (244). These concepts, for Williams, are collaboration, multimodality, publishing, and sampling and remixing. Williams widens the conceptual framework for creative writing as imagined by Goldsmith (who is almost exclusively concerned with sampling and remixing) as well as a print-oriented understanding of creative writing by including other concepts through which to orient the digitally inflected creative writing classroom and, by extension, the scope of the field. Important to recognize here is that this is a shift not only from page to screen, but also, perhaps more importantly, from genre to process. As digital conceptions of craft emerge, in other words, we see not only new and hybrid genres materialize, but that *concepts* through which strategies for constructing a text are privileged over the reproduction of particular conventions. As Williams explains, "The first two categories [of his classifications] mark ways in which digital media offer changes to activities, such as collaboration and response or publishing and distribution, that have always been central to creative writing pedagogy. The second two areas of multimodality and sampling and remixing are substantively different from the traditional focus of the creative writing classroom, but worth exploring in terms of contemporary creative writing courses" (251).

Williams's essay outlines the classroom application of these categories. But most significant here is the way in which digital media—and the construction of a text within digital environments—brings forth an understanding that the reproduction of genre need not be the default condition of the field. His essay points to the ways in which creative writing pedagogy can adapt to the construction of a text across digital platforms and that this necessarily entails addressing issues of process as they become relevant to the construction of particular digital texts. In his essay "Creative Writing and Process Pedagogy," Mayers claims this requires the rejection of "the twin notions that, on the one hand, writers' processes are too mysterious to describe, and on the other hand, that the attempt to describe and analyze writers' processes is harmful or destructive to those processes" (43). Including digital environments in understanding what it means to produce imaginative texts, in other words, inevitably requires addressing how a text works as it integrates the several modes available through digital media. Because these environments require the explicit engagement of multiple modes, they inevitably require addressing the process of engaging those modes. And they establish new disciplinary relationships.

"Writers working in new media," writes Scott Rettberg in "Electronic Literature as Digital Humanities," "are both creating discrete literary experiences and testing the chemistry of a particular creative admixture of writing and technological apparatus" (129). This, according to Rettberg, situates electronic literature—the construction of an imaginative text across different media—in a unique position among its disciplinary counterparts in the academy. As Rettberg points out in his comprehensive review of work being done at the intersection of literature and technology:

Electronic literature has emerged as a distinctive digital humanities field in its own right, with conferences, festivals, and a growing body of dissertations, monographs, and edited collections addressing the subject. Electronic literature functions as a field of digital humanities research on a number of different levels, each with their own defining characteristics. These include:

1. Creative digital media practice in electronic literature;
2. The development of specific platforms for creative practices in digital media;

3. Theoretical work and analysis works of electronic literature to build new understandings of contemporary textuality and "digital vernaculars";

4. The establishment of networked scholarly practices, digital publications, research infrastructures, and social networks particular to the digital research environment; and

5. Meta analysis and visualization research based on electronic literature metadata. (128)

As I describe in Chapter 2, if imaginative writers wish to sandwich their readers into their texts by integrating into those texts readers' sensory participation (as interactive digital storytelling allows), then one consideration the *process* category of digital creative writing studies brings to light is the need to develop a sustained theoretical approach toward the sensory and interpretive immersion that craft becomes. While the figure of reader-as-writer is hardly new to scholarship, the recruitment of technologies that materially require the reader to occupy/construct that duality is. Creative writing studies in the twenty-first century can use the digital environment in which this duality takes places as a way of asking imaginative writers to begin examining/ imagining writing beyond the sensation provided by lines of language on the page and how participation with a variety of sensation may provide new ways of understanding craft as a synthesis of readers' affect and participation in an unfolding narrative. Rettberg here outlines how this is a project that not only requires a fluid understanding of genre, since it works toward building "new understandings of contemporary textuality," but also a nuanced understanding of how that process engages those multiple modes throughout the writing process—and puts creative writing in conversation with other fields in the academy.

As creative writing studies begins to mount such arguments—to make space for a fluid understanding of genre that takes into account a closer understanding of the process of producing an imaginative text—the discipline takes one step toward networked ways of knowing and how creative writing stands to become a field involved more explicitly with the production of knowledge (about the construction of imaginative texts, digital, multimodal, or monomodal) rather than exclusively the reproduction of particular genres.

To answer the questions "are blogs creative nonfiction?" and "can a writer determine what a text will look like as she drafts it across multiple modes?" requires considering genre/form and process as concepts in concert with each other. What genres emerge as writers draft texts across multiple modes? What forces are already at work on those genres and processes? What does it mean to consider those forces alongside new and emerging ones? The answers to such questions would situate creative writing studies as a discipline intimately bound up with the production of knowledge. As Rettberg points out above, "the chemistry of a particular admixture of writing and technological apparatus" positions creative writing alongside other disciplines—composition studies primarily and literary studies—as it prepares answers and explores new configurations of "networked scholarly practices."

Recall Franzen's points in *The Krauss Project*:

America in 2013 is . . . another weakened empire telling itself stories of its exceptionalism while it drifts toward apocalypse of some sort, fiscal or epidemiological, climatic-environmental or thermonuclear. Our Far Left may hate religion and think we coddle Israel, our Far Right may hate illegal immigrants and think we coddle black people, and nobody may know how the economy is supposed to work now that our manufacturing jobs have gone overseas, but the actual substance of our daily lives is total electronic distraction. . . . What we can all agree to do instead is to deliver ourselves to the cool new media and technologies, to Steve Jobs and Mark Zuckerberg and Jeff Bezos, and to let them profit at our expense. Our situation looks quite a bit like Vienna's in 1910, except that newspaper technology (telephone, telegraph, the high speed printing press) has been replaced by digital technology and Viennese charm by American coolness. (14)

In *The Rhetoric of Cool: Composition Studies and New Media*, Jeff Rice is "interested in how cool functions as a rhetorical act. [His] interests, however, are [mostly] concerned with how cool shapes an emerging technological apparatus we are living, working, studying, and teaching within" (2). In constructing a generalizable rhetoric of cool as it shapes such conditions, Rice points a way toward understanding composing and writing in electronic environments. New rhetorical gestures emerge: appropriation, juxtaposition, nonlinearity, imagery—all new ways of making meaning emerge in the landscape of composition studies, which also reorient the ways in which we understand the rhetorical possibilities available for any writer composing in electronic environments. Requiring a fluid understanding of genre and process in digital environments, which likewise reorients the field of creative writing studies and points it toward the production of knowledge devoted to how imaginative texts survive within such a technological apparatus, leads inevitably to considering how creative writing is defined according to its institutional practice and disciplinary identity, which I will attend to in the next chapter.

But first consider the ways in which the above authors work alongside the word "cool." For Franzen, it is a superficial signifier, one that addresses a reductive understanding of being fashionable—of not being critical enough. Rice's definition asks us to examine how "cool new media" generate new rhetorical gestures. For writers like Marshal McLuhan and Paul Miller, cool media engage several modes and several senses simultaneously, requiring active participation on the part of the audience and, I would add, critical intervention on the part of the scholar devoted to understanding what it means to write within them. As creative writing studies maneuvers through its digital turn, these arguments highlight the ways in which the field is mastered by print-oriented understandings of genre. Digital craft criticism points to a new kind of work emerging in creative writing studies—one that impresses upon us the importance of process in that field, especially as it incorporates digital technologies—and one that moves the field closer to producing knowledge and criticism regarding the effects of these technologies on the actual texts they shape. Identifying the role technology plays in the construction of an imaginative text, in other words, helps scholars of creative writing studies situate the way in which all imaginative writing is technological, which frees us to see the ways in which technologies are already at work when we talk about writing, how genre works as an extension of that technology, the ways in which "cool new media" bring that to light and present new ways speaking back to the cultural conditions in which genres are always imagined and (re) invented.

5

Fenceless Neighbors: On Composition, Creative Writing, and Emerging Institutional Practices

In March 2001, Wendy Bishop found herself in the midst of what would later be referred to as "the new theory wars." Composition studies, while grappling with what had been up to that point the field's central object of study—first year composition—had widened in its scholarship to include research on how philosophical, rhetorical, and cultural studies research methods intersected with the teaching and study of writing. Rhetorical analysis, ontological turns, and empirical research brought into composition journals arguments that, according to Bishop (who served at this time as chair of the Conference on College Composition and Communication), problematic shifts away from foundational theories and identities of the field, specifically among them: expressivism. As John Trimbur points out in his article, "Changing the Question: Should Writing Be Studied?," a particular current began to gain momentum at the turn of the century: "The significance of this current, I believe, is that it raises fundamental questions about the identity and activity of writing teachers and theorists all over again. Only this time the question is not 'Can writing be taught?' or 'How can writing be learned?' but 'Should Writing be Studied?'" (18).

Bishop proposed an answer to that question in her article, "Places to Stand: The Reflective Writer-Teacher-Writer in Composition," from a special issue of *College Composition and Communication*, edited by Joe Harris, dedicated to the theme of "Teaching Writing Creatively," and inquiring into the "nexus of composition studies and creative writing." In that article she speaks back to what she sees as the marginalization of expressivism specifically and the status of the "writer-teacher-writer" (as opposed to the usual "teacher-scholar") identity politics of the field more generally. In short, Bishop's article aims to clarify problematic dismissals of expressivism in the field, citing misrepresentation, especially of the work of Donald Murray and Peter Elbow. In this way, Bishop's answer to the question "Should Writing be Studied?" stands to include addressing the ways in which writers are always implicated in what it means to even ask that question in the first place, something Murray and Elbow's work took seriously and revealed as theoretically and practically complex. The field of composition studies, in other words, is comprised of research questions that stem from the indissoluble relationship between writer and text, which requires, for Bishop, a place at the table for voice, community, and reflection in all modes of study within composition, even as those modes widened to include new methodologies for the study of writing. Veering away from such concerns, her argument implies, necessarily means transforming the field in problematic ways—essentially, to move full circle to the first chapter of this book, to abandon human imagination as it can be understood as an intellectual and creative mode of expression, for the sake of empirical, or rhetorical, or cultural, understandings of writing.

In his response to Bishop's article, Gary Olson calls such a position "the death of composition as an intellectual discipline." In that article (of that title), he attacks Bishop's perceived marginality and characterization of academic prose as that which should invite a general audience. Bishop, citing scholarship from Lynn Bloom, Mike Rose, Lad Tobin, Kathleen Blake Yancey, and several others, argues for a kind of composition scholarship that provides accessibility for undergraduates and those who wish to enter the field. Olson, finding this position problematic, asks, "Since when is scholarship in any field written with undergraduates in mind? Do we now have to certify that nuclear physicists write in such a way that sophomores can 'enter and participate' in their scholarly discussions" (37)? For what it's worth, Olson's argument seems at least a little motivated by Bishop's usage of his own work as the kind of work emerging in composition studies that she finds problematic. Bishop writes:

> Who appropriates what voice and for what purposes? . . . I had to ask myself two nights ago, exactly what this sentence (not from *CCC* but from a composition journal) means? And why it was made: "While Pratt's notion of contact zones has been useful in interrogating how teachers

exercise power and authority, especially in the multi cultural classroom, some compositionists have tended to deploy it in such a way as to defend a kind of liberal pluralism, thereby subverting attempts to come to terms with the truly colonizing effects of the pedagogical scenario." For me, the sentence, I realized, had no clothes, and no heart (no organs at all, no human substance) no place for the interested writer/teacher/writer in me to stand. (26)

Olson ultimately attacks Bishop's position by virtue of her framing this issue as a matter of style—why must this author write in an obtuse fashion?—but, perhaps anticipating this, Bishop provides a clarification later in that same passage: "When I say such a sentence has no clothes, I am not being merely personal, nor am I on the attack. I am on the inquiry, asking Who—what figure of author—is speaking? To what figure of reader? For what social purpose (in the society of *CCC*)? And where in this tactical, strategic, figurative, social landscape is there a place for [the writer/teacher/writer]" (26)?

Olson ultimately describes the issue as a matter of ideological struggle, the evolution of competing methods regarding how to study writing, which, as Trimbur observes, is a question that stands to see composition (and creative writing) into its next iteration, its next institutional identity. Olson points out that

in every discipline there is hegemonic struggle over the identity of that discipline. That is, one group of like-minded individuals attempts to further its vision of the field, while other groups do the same. For example, throughout the 70s the people that we've come to call "cognitivists" and those we've come to call "expressivists" battled between themselves over how the field should be defined, and in doing so they both maintained tight control over the means of dissemination of scholarship. (37)

As Joseph Moxley puts it in his preface to *Creative Writing in America*, "There is evidence that our discipline is preparing to undergo a paradigm shift, a period of self-reflexiveness in which we question our theories and practices" (xi). When Wendy Bishop tries to steer composition studies toward those questions, more toward the emerging methodologies of creative writing, she does so by centering her argument on the metaphorical "head vs the heart." She wants composition studies to always maintain its understanding of that indissoluble relationship between writer and text—its fundamentally human character. Olson wants to point out that there are several methodologies through which to do so. And, as Moxley forecasted in 1989, creative writing has taken on the work of questioning its pedagogical (Ritter, Vanderslice) and disciplinary (Donnelly) practices. To enter those discussions as they begin to take on concerns related to the digital humanities, requires, I argue, a set of particularly concrete approaches, which I will organize in this chapter according to the methodological, pedagogical, and disciplinary identity beginning to emerge across that vast terrain creative writing studies stands to contribute to. As such, this concluding chapter offers specific findings across these three areas: within the methodological, I incorporate a range of emerging practices and the framework we use for examining those practices; within the pedagogical I move toward a kind of teaching not necessarily framed by the workshop method, and within the emerging disciplinary identity I define the paradigm shift that digital creative writing studies signifies as well as the ways it stands to contribute to the production of knowledge in the academy, specifically within the digital humanities.

I begin with Bishop and Olson's exchange at the start of the century in order to frame those concerns more largely in the tectonic shift that undergirds most discussions of how the digital humanities inflects the fields of study within it—fields of study that, of course, serve the larger questions of what it means to be human. As creative writing moves into concerns regarding how developing technologies are changing the scene of imaginative writing, then, I want to urge from the outset that I am not abandoning that humanistic mission. Like Bishop, I want research and the production of knowledge in creative writing studies to serve that larger project—and like Olson, I want to advocate for several methods to bring us there. Put another way, echoing Katherine Haake, who "argues for a shift within the discipline that would respond to student difference and allow for reconceiving creative writing as a practice that may take many forms of value in the lives and education of our students," this chapter examines the repercussions of a digital creative writing studies in terms of methodology, pedagogy, and disciplinary identity, in order not only to situate creative writing's place in the digital humanities, but also to demonstrate how a diverse set of methodological conditions can help serve our students, our writers, and our readers in order to extend the project of making the study of creative writing more fully human.

Methodological

Susan Miller's chapter in Olson's edited collection, *Rhetoric and Composition as Intellectual Work*, provides a valuable place to start. In that essay, "Writing Studies as a Mode of Inquiry," Miller argues for "a strategically calculated descriptor that can assure its future development, as well as general agreement over the particular set of intellectual questions that such a descriptor entails" which she calls "writing studies" (41). This field, which also signifies its content, for Miller, examines

> the personal and social/material circumstances in which [texts] are produced . . . engages both historical and contemporary concerns, addresses acts of writing and their products as evidence of a particularly crucial cultural work in which a whole text offers an intellectual/expressive act that intersects circulating discursive practices. This inquiry does not detach "popular" from "high" texts, nor does it separate "ordinary" from "creative" writers on the basis of relative visionary talent or levels of access to the ethical and economic status requisite to authorship. But it does define culture as a conjunction of specific acts of composition and their resulting texts. (42, original emphasis)

Consider this next to Bishop's claim in *Released into Language* that "creative writing needs to be responsive to theoretical and pedagogical changes taking place in literary studies and composition studies (not to mention cultural studies, feminist studies, and linguistics)" and we can see that not only is examining creative writing in light of its digital practices a way to illuminate those practices, but also, and perhaps more importantly, one way in which creative writing stands to work with its neighboring fields. Miller's understanding of "writing studies" articulated above puts creative writing in dialogue with its neighboring fields in English studies. It methodologically has more to say to its colleagues.

Citing Tim Mayers, Dianne Donnelly's *Establishing Creative Writing Studies an Academic Discipline* sees framing digital concerns in light of how the emerging discipline stands to contribute to growing bodies of knowledge:

> Mayers (2009: 225) offers opportunities for scholars in creative writing studies to intersect with compositionists as a means of "explor[ing] the implications of new electronic forms of text distribution." Beyond this

intersection, we witness the forward movement of creative writing studies as creative writing teachers embrace and incorporate more technological literacy skills (literary hypertext, digital narratives, podcasts and such) into their course design. While we witness a decline in printed books and material (and appreciate that a symbiotic relationship exists between the printed and digital text), we see creativity and technology merge in ways that (1) transcend academic disciplines and the digital culture of universities and (2) consider—for our students as creative artists in the 21st century—new audiences, relative skills and practical opportunities in writing in digital environments.

As part of its ongoing collaboration with composition studies, a digital arm of creative writing studies, as I have shown in previous chapters, can of course provide the lines of inquiry Donnelly points to above, but also incorporate others: ethnographic research of online writing communities; imaginative digital work as a form of collaboration; inquiry into digital practices; interdisciplinary work with visual arts and performing arts; even the production of scholarly journals. These are all important directions that a digital arm of creative writing studies, in keeping with Bishop's notion that the study of writing should always include the relationship between a writer and her text, can use to address the growing body of knowledge surrounding new media and creative writing. In these ways (and more) creative writing studies stands to speak back to writing studies and the knowledge produced within that field. Again, as Donnelly explains:

> What we need to know about creative writing and research is how to facilitate a better understanding of creative writing's particular modes of research. While academic research methodologies have been clearly defined, creative writing "needs to develop its own domain-specific methodologies" (Dean and Smith, 2006: 5). With full control of its own research methods, the discipline should define "under what conditions meaning is to be treated as knowledge or as the acquisition of knowledge" (Niklas Luhmann qtd. in Reilly, 2002) rather than to have these conditions awkwardly shaped by traditional university research standards. As creative writing researchers we need "to promote a better understanding of where our particular kind of activity 'fits', and to claim appropriate support for our high productivity in this area." (Meehan, 2010)

Examination of digital practices, theories, and pedagogies can of course begin this work. But it can also introduce new directions for the field to consider as more and more scholars of creative writing begin to take on those diverse projects. To frame it as a question: Do the ways in which digital environments provide occasion for creative writing scholars to (re)investigate issues of pedagogy, subjectivity/authority, and process/genre require the field to recalibrate its very disciplinary identity? If, as Trimbur puts it, the question is now "Should Writing be Studied?" (as opposed to reproduced), does this require the methodological reorganization of creative writing studies at large?

On the one hand, yes. How can creative writing programs that work toward including the production of multimodal and digitally born texts within its disciplinary boundaries continue to organize themselves according to the three major—print-oriented—genres that have so far defined the field? The development of new digitally born genres would, of course, require that creative writing programs consider new ways of at least framing those courses—as either at the service of new genres (like Robert Coover's Hypertext Fiction Workshop) or the processes through which student writers will explore and construct texts (like U-Mass-Amherst's Experimental Writing Workshop or Kenneth Goldsmith's Uncreative Writing class). The striking way in which such courses stick out from the regular business of creative writing at large signifies that, at the most extreme level, a break from traditional institutional practices would be within the realm of possibility.

But on the other hand, do a diverse set of methods—and a range of questions within which a discipline constructs its knowledge—necessarily herald the end of (disciplinary) times? I will actually return to this question in the final section of this chapter, but for the time being, it suffices to say that the diverse range of methodologies that emerge when we incorporate consideration of digital environments in the construction of imaginative texts primarily provide the emerging discipline of creative writing studies with a way of engaging with what the construction of imaginative texts have always engaged in: other forms, aesthetic debates; the development of new materials does, of course, make new options available for the artist, but, as I hope I have shown over the course of this argument, that isn't a process of negation more than it is a process of affirmation and exploration. What this means in terms of the kind of knowledge digital creative writing studies stands to produce I will say more about in the final section.

But to return to the methodological issue at hand: a digital arm of creative writing studies contributes to the overall body of knowledge that writing studies aims to develop and, remembering Wendy Bishop, should always be part of a larger project that aims to demystify the creative process. As a field whose methodological question—how does one write a poem or story?—largely hinges on conventional (highly formal practice and conventions) as well as experimentation (new ways in which those forms are inflected within particular historical moments), the ways in which a digital turn within creative writing is already taking place provides us with the answer Trimbur poses (should writing be studied?). The answer, to perhaps oversimplify it, is that we have already begun to feel the shift happen beneath our feet. Questions emerge around that sensation. Their answers will be formed through a methodological richness that works toward understanding in a deeper and more sustained way, as this book has begun to show, how the digital inflects the creative—and what this means for creative writers.

More specifically and, perhaps, more immediately, the practices of creative writers working within and across emerging media proliferate considerably. A short taxonomy of the practices that this book has encountered, practices that span the four concrete ways in which I've imagined digital creative writing studies—process, genre, authority, and institutional practice—shows not only the ways in which new practices develop alongside emerging technologies, but also the major ways in which naming and employing those practices asks the field to reorient itself. *Nonlinearity* and *intertextuality* as we inherit them from hypertext and employ them in multimodal contexts that reshape *generic boundaries* and recruit *appropriation* emerge as the first few visible writing practices that can help creative writing studies stabilize its disciplinary tools while at the same time, as acknowledging those practices asks us to do, develop significant research methodologies that continue the long-term project of historicizing, theorizing, and sustaining deep examination of how these technologically mediated practices inform the process of producing an imaginative text.

These practices will always be deeply human, which is to say that they will be employed by writers, no matter how visible they allow the technological imprint on their work to be, who will be using those tools in order to express and acknowledge the human ache that has always fueled our richest imaginative literature. Consider the cyberfeminism of Jackson's "Patchwork Girl," the technologically enabled self of Monson's *Vanishing Point*, the long-term childhood literacy project of Pullinger and Joseph's *Inanimate Alice*. These are works uninterested in pretending that the work of the imagination is not technologically mediated. And they acknowledge that the act of symbolic expression has always been technologically enabled. How do we understand not only how to use these practices more effectively (which will, of course, be a socially constructed and ongoing project for creative writing scholars), but also how we understand what it means—as humans—to use them?

Put another way: our methods are, or should be, equally human as well. In order to flesh out what possibilities (and/or peril) lie in wait as creative writers take into account the variety of ways in which technology—not to mention other material factors—impacts the process of creative invention, creative writing scholars stand at a moment in our scholarship when we can consider seriously Adeline Koh's call for a "new wave" of digital humanities scholarship that has "humanistic questions at its core—because the humanities, centrally, is the study of how people process and document human cultures and ideas, and is fundamentally about asking critical questions of the methods used to document and process." Or, as Jim Brown explains in "Writing with Machines: Data and Process in Taroko Gorge": "Any creative endeavor emerges from collaboration, from the various readers who comment on drafts to the inspiration we draw from other creative works. . . . From writing spaces to desks to favorite notebooks and pens to methods of revision to the observance of linguistic constraints, writers construct and author their writing situations. Much like a computer program, the human writing process is an authored set of procedures, created for a particular set of circumstances" (132). As we author those methodologies that examine the set of forces that I have shown are at work on the creative writer when we set that figure in relation to the enabling and determining factors at work on her processes, then we inevitably enrich not only what it means to study creative writing specifically, but English studies at large.

Pedagogy

Because technology is so often seen as a tool at a writer's disposal—rather than, as I hope this book shows, a dynamic force at work on the creative process—digital tools in the creative writing classroom have been the institutional practice most often written about and discussed. In *Creative Writing Pedagogies for the Twenty-first Century*, Bronwyn T. Williams shows the ways in which digital tools extend from the print-oriented practices traditionally associated with workshop pedagogy. And in Jake Adam York's chapter from Graeme Harper and Jeri Kroll's edited collection, *Creative Writing Studies: Practice, Research, and Pedagogy*, titled "Let Stones Speak: New Media Remediation in the Poetry Writing Classroom," those tools are at the service of a pedagogy that provides avenues into understanding the sonic properties of poetics and the material conditions through which poetry is read and written, stating that he "wants to use new media software to encourage students to place their own senses, all of them, in the service of reading and in the service of writing" (24). By recruiting audio editor software, York explains, students can visualize language in ways that we haven't been able to do before, making visual the aural and identifying the ways in which the senses can be understood in terms of each other, allowing writers to visualize their work in illuminating ways.

At stake for both these creative writing scholars, each working through the expressive capacity of new media in the creative writing classroom, is a particular investment in the simultaneous valuation of old forms and new ways. As Williams points out, creative writing seems to be at a moment in its development as a discipline in which its rootedness in print traditions and simultaneous implication in emerging technologies stands to position the creative writing classroom as a space where a range of pedagogical action can be taken. I bring this up in order to say that despite its stronghold on much of creative writing's pedagogy, the workshop model, in an age of mediated texts and writers, stands to be transformed or synthesized with the new models through which creative writing is taught. But not without considerable attention paid to the ways in which print practices continue to exert their forces on those spaces.

For example, in "Creative Writing for New Media," Amy Letter states that "teaching writing for new media is [not] a world apart from teaching traditional creative writing. There are more similarities than differences, and most of the differences have corollaries to traditional course practices" (188). Pointing out that teaching poetry in the creative writing classroom is not synonymous with teaching grammar, though the two obviously overlap, using new media in the classroom, according to Letter, is not synonymous with teaching the technology. She demonstrates that teaching creative writing for new media, however, can take students and student projects to new places: "To make sure that everyone achieves the maximum benefit from the course," she says, "students must work at or near the edge of their skill set: every assignment should ask the students to consciously identify something they don't yet know how to do, whether that's creating a hyperlink, using a specific program for the first time, or creating a certain effect, and accomplish that new task as a part of the larger project" (182).

In York's class, software is used for poets to visualize spoken language in order to inform their choices as poets. In Letter's class, a variety of digital media are recruited in order to provide alternative ways into writing poetry or fiction that consciously reflect the medium through which they are constructed. For example, Letter's assignments range from "creating an artificial persona online" (through Twitter, Tumblr, Blogger) to nonlinear, kinetic story writing. The genres are loosely imagined in Letter's classroom and the students are encouraged to use new media as a way of not only reimagining old genres, but also in finding new combinations. Rob Wittig and Mark C Marino's chapter from the same collection, "Acting Out: Netprov in the Classroom," identifies a new genre, "netprov" ("stories created in existing networked media that are collaborative and improvised in real time"), and works through a pedagogical model for effectively teaching it.

Such developments branch creative writing away from the workshop model, since the medium, in a technologically inflected understanding of creative writing, will always require discussion in any context that seeks to examine how the effect of an imaginative piece works. The medium's effect on the craft, that is, as it develops a particular effect in a particular element of poem or story necessarily requires its own discussion, veering the technologically mediated creative writing class away from the workshop model, where print-normed notions of craft are often static and require, arguably, less discussion time. However, perhaps more importantly, we see that two paths begin to emerge, given such distinctions. In the first, creative practice is *informed* by new media. Poetry in York's class, for example, remains safely within the confines of its genre and the students remain safely within the confines of their status as poets. Their practice is informed by what they learn regarding the materiality of language through sound editing software. Much of creative writing practice and pedagogy can theoretically work along these lines even in an age of emerging media and closer scholarly attention to the ways in which technology mediates creative production. Business, in a sense, can continue as usual.

The second path, however, follows creative practice as it is *transformed* by new media. New genres emerge alongside new practices, shaped by new and emerging tools, all of which contribute to an understanding of digital literature and creative writing's place in its production. To work across the variety of modes made available through digital technology, to work through the various ways such technologies recruit subject positions and perpetuate ideological stances, and to advance that work along the lines that one would call "experimental" in a carefully theorized way presents not only a new kind of methodological orientation for academic creative writers to work through, but also a set of new practices so overwhelmingly proliferated in our culture as to suggest the possibility of developing entire creative writing programs devoted to the production of imaginative texts that take into account the technological stages on which their drama is set. It is not impossible to imagine a creative writing program that will explore what these advancements mean. In the tradition of all past literacy crises, I am tempted to call such emergence a "crossroads."

But I won't. Because it is, I contend, more productively imagined as a pedagogical dialectic that enriches the field of creative writing. On the one hand, examining creative writing pedagogy in light of technological mediation means simply admitting that we have always been technologically mediated, that a poem or a story is a form of technology and we can continue teaching those forms consciously into the foreseeable future; on the other hand, it means reinventing the classroom space in order to account for new forms and processes as they emerge across digital spaces. I know this sounds like I'm trying to have it two ways. But I am presenting this dialectic as a starting point for creative writing, an axis along which research and pedagogy can continually orbit each other as the field continues into the twenty-first century. To address the ways in which print-oriented craft works to particular effect in poetry, fiction, and creative nonfiction alongside the ways in which digitally mediated work is obviously one direction such a dialectic could take, but there are others as well. How do stories work alongside other fields in the arts, like music or painting? What can poetry learn from performance art? How can we develop multimodal understandings that attend to the possibilities in mixing mediums that exist outside the scope of digital media? What does it mean to teach creative production along these lines?

Identifying the ways in which print-oriented notions of craft refract through digital and multimodal notions of craft or constructing new wholly digital notions of craft shows us how dynamic creative writing pedagogy can be as it takes into account the ways in which it is technologically mediated. It is our role as scholar-teachers, as I hope this argument has made clear, to work within, across, and through such dialectics in the fashioning of theories and practices that continually inform our pedagogy.

Disciplinary identity

"Research into our processes and practices," Dianne Donnelly observes in *Establishing Creative Writing Studies as an Academic Discipline*, "leads us to consider what else is possible in the workshop space, to suggest how we might best assess student writing and to embrace (among others) multimodal approaches and new conceptual spaces for digital compositions" (124). Embracing those conceptual spaces—their theoretical and practical dialectics—leads that field, as this book begins to identify, toward not only nongenre defined understandings of what it means to study creative writing, but perhaps more importantly, renewed relationships with the larger sociopolitical and cultural context that surrounds it. "In the UK and Australian creative writing programs," Donnelly further points out, "graduate students . . . are guided 'to be conscious . . . of context, looking backward in order to look forward—to perceive, in effect, what needs to be done creatively at this point in their culture' (Kroll, 2008: 9). It's a recursive process in which research 'begins before-during/after practice, aided by ideas generated by practice, in order to produce new knowledge' (Kroll, 2008: 9). The process incorporates a research question at the onset (or early in the process) of writing creatively, so that the critical exploration intersects at many points with the creative process" (124).

Paul Dawson, in *Creative Writing and the New Humanities*, addresses this in terms of the public intellectual, that public figure uniquely suited to provide the critical and creative voice in a fragmented culture. Creative writing programs, along the lines of his argument, stand to produce such intellectuals and it is my contention that through the range of methodological, pedagogical, and theoretical sets of concerns that this book has begun to address, the inclusion of digital creative writing studies provides creative writing the chance to do such work. In other words, creative writing should be a discipline uniquely qualified, as Kroll puts it, "to perceive, in effect, what needs to be done creatively at this point in their culture" (9). In an age of paradigm-shifting technological emergence, this requires at the very least the growth of the field to further address those elements at stake in a technologically mediated understanding of creative writing that I have outlined throughout this argument. On the other end of that spectrum, though, growth in this direction could also lead to a total recalibration of what it means to compose imaginative texts at a moment when technological mediation is so widespread. More on that later.

But for now, I am particularly interested in how this provides a renewed relationship between the neighboring fields of creative writing and composition. Composition's imagination has always been a place where, as I discuss in Chapter 1, we store our hopes and dreams for a discipline in which creativity and humanity are given space to interanimate each other and insofar as critical-creative composition has emerged as a way to understand form/disciplinarity and transformation as two major threads of what it means to use imagination in the composition classroom, examining those practices next to creative writing shows us just how different those two fields have become at this point in their history. Over the course of this book, that is, I have attempted to imagine their relationship in the context of new and emerging media and the concerns they ask us to address. But what does it show us about the relationship between composition and creative writing studies?

Beyond the obvious—that composition (perhaps ironically) emerges as the more progressive discipline, at least the discipline for whom "creative" is not necessarily synonymous with exclusive notions of form—it is a relationship that thrives on openness *and* exclusivity. Collections like *Creative Writing Pedagogy in the Twenty-first Century* and *Creative Writing in the Digital Age* remind us that these two fields do provide each other with innovative ways of imagining the other, but also that they work through a variety of (*sometimes* overlapping) methodological territory. That is to say that the ongoing dialogue between these two areas of writing studies, where the theoretical and pedagogical practices of examining writing as a technologically mediated process, presents to creative writing studies the possibilities of new directions, at the same time as it uniquely positions writing studies at large to continue developing as a field that, as creative writing enters the conversation, contributes to a body of knowledge invested in what it means to conduct humanistic research in an age of digital production.

The relationship between the literary object and the digital humanities has so far been defined by the historical and theoretical orientation provided by the interpretive critical apparatus of literature as a subfield of English studies. Jennifer Glaser and Laura R. Micciche, in "Digitizing English," put it this way (and it is worth quoting at length):

> DH as ideology and practice can help us challenge what counts as English in at least two ways. First, it provides inspiration for revising English so it rotates not around literary production and reception but around practices of making. One possible model, for example, could be organized around writing practices. This focus would make possible multidirectional, cross-sectional relations between and among subfields, all of which cohere around writing in one way or another. To foreground writing relations among English department members is to make powerful our collective emotional and intellectual attachments to language, its transcription, diversity, and effects. It is also to organize collectives around an activity—writing—rather than around subject matter, methods, or theory. Speaking of writing practices instead of discrete areas like literature, creative writing, or cultural studies insists on our entanglements with one another rather than suppressing them in the continual struggle for a fair take of diminishing resources. It also subverts the division between production, associated with rhetorical studies, and consumption, linked to literary studies, that has long plagued English department workings.

Glaser and Micciche use the digital humanities (DH) as a way to organize the work of English departments around practices of making, which brings them to a conclusion in which such a vision for English studies at large requires the collapsing of boundaries, if not the increasing production of scholarship that works at the intersection(s) of subfields. Disciplinary identity of English departments, within such a scheme, would remarkably resemble those emerging methodologies developing at the intersection of composition, creative writing, and the digital humanities as I have outlined them in the argument of this book. In what follows, I will demonstrate how the particular triangulation of composition, creative writing studies, and the digital humanities helps provide English departments the full disciplinary richness these developments seek out.

Fenceless neighbors: Composition, creative writing studies, and the digital humanities

Consider the hermeneutic privileging that Jeff Rice points out in his *College English* article "Occupying the Digital Humanities":

> The loosely affiliated networks of literary scholars, writing specialists, historians, and librarians working on non-print-based approaches to their disciplines often feel like an umbrella covering disparate work in varied disciplines under the rubric of being digital. What often unites such distinct work, however, is the notion of hermeneutics; that is, the practice of interpretation. Hermeneutics often dominate digital humanities scholarship because scholars drawn to this type of work carry over its application from rhetorical, literary, and cultural studies in order to interpret and explain phenomena in digital spaces. (360)

Rice seeks an understanding of digital humanities work that is *not* an interpretive treatment of digital texts, but rather an application "of new logics and new communicative methods" (361). Drawing from Roland Barthes' definition of myths and mythologizing, Rice claims that "given its umbrella-like status and quest for alternative approaches to print-based scholarship, the digital humanities, it seems, might welcome Barthes's notion of mythologizing the myth as an alternative digital practice in order to further advance the cause of digital humanities work" (361). In other words, reimagining the digital humanities as a space in which understanding digital artifacts as acts within larger communicative acts does not mean the same things as interpreting those texts. It is instead an act that asks writers to inhabit critical and creative "logics" that work toward the production rather than the interpretation of digital texts. The digital humanities, Rice argues, would be an opportune space for such logics to take place.

This is what I take Glaser and Micciche to mean by "thinking with DH (digital humanities)" as a way to reconceive academic labor and its purposes. Thinking with DH allows scholars across the digital humanities to build networks that have the potential to generate surprising and valuable collectives. For example, they also point out that "the curatorial dimensions of creative and critical work are exuberantly evident in the work of online archivists like Charles Bernstein, Kenneth Goldsmith, and Craig Dworkin" and their work with PennSound and the Electronic Poetry Center at the State University of New York "marries the work of a traditional scholarly archive to a more radical aesthetic and curatorial project—serving a global community of poets, critics, and teachers while also inventing new audiences for poetry who can engage it as a performative art rather than one that exists exclusively on the page" (203). Thinking with DH, Glaser and Micciche point out, requires the kind of consolidation we heard Paul Miller advocating in earlier chapters of this book: the combining of the critical, creative, and pedagogical within a paradigm that does not ask them to do interpretive work, but rather establish productive approaches.

Glaser and Micciche contextualize such an approach by illustrating how thinking with DH provides a way to organize the field of English studies at large. They argue that thinking with DH challenges what traditionally counts as English in two ways: it orients the work of the English department around "practices of making" which establishes our work as an activity rather than— or as well as, depending on your area of study—a hermeneutic enterprise perpetually emphasizing difference through disciplinary identity (literature, creative writing, and composition studies). Similarly to the thinking Rice advocates, thinking with DH in an English department challenges the thinking and assemblages there through a recalibration of what it means to examine communication and expression given the technological shifts taking place around the disciplines of English studies. Thinking with DH unthreads our traditional ways of knowing (what Rice would say are hermeneutic) and professional classifications (literary studies, creative writing, and composition), constructing an area of study that would make possible multidirectional, cross-sectional relations between and among subfields all of which are perpetually investigating what it means to write across dramatically and continually shifting territory.

Composition and creative writing's relationship in such a configuration, I argue, should lead such directions. If we imagine the work of English studies to be the production of writers—scholarly, creative, public—and the delivery of a refined training that requires those writers to consider the material and ideological forces at work on the production of a text so that the read/write cycle is informed by the (f)act of writing, then the production of such writers—or, put more modestly, the opportunities we can present to students who wish to explore those writerly identities and practices—would, naturally, be happening at the nexus of those fields developing research within those areas. At this stage of the game, in the second decade of the twenty-first century, that research is produced under what Susan Miller would call "Writing Studies" and what others might call the productive collaboration between the subfields of composition, rhetoric, and creative writing.

I have argued in this book that the particular triangulation of composition studies, creative writing studies, and the digital humanities provides a powerful way of revisiting the relationship between composition and creative writing as it has emerged in the later half of the twentieth century. We can begin to recognize new practices—nonlinearity, intertextuality, genre shifting, appropriation—and situate them as signs of a techno-cultural shift that asks us to consider the ways in which emerging technologies shape the production of imaginative texts. In terms of disciplinary identity, when placed within the broader context of the shifting boundaries of English studies at large, especially as the digital humanities has asked the field to reorient itself, the particular partnership between composition and creative writing carries with it the potential for an even more transformative effect: the orientation of creative writing studies as a subfield situated to "think with" the digital humanities as well as "speak back" to it. While the relationships across subfields within English studies steadies itself according to the disciplinary effects of integrating digital humanities methods into the examination of its object of study, a digitally inflected understanding of creative writing studies—one that emphasizes methods of production over interpretation—positions students to talk about a range of texts and the processes by which to produce them in ways

English studies has yet to fully investigate. That is to say, as Rice points out, the digital humanities have so far been shaped by hermeneutic approaches toward the production of knowledge. But while creative writing establishes itself as a discipline within the academy and with its own evolving methodological approach toward its object of study—the production of an imaginative text— it becomes a powerful voice in the discussions about the nonhermeneutic approaches toward the production of knowledge, or what Glaser and Micciche call "practices of making." What will this emerging voice within this evolving discipline say?

In his conclusion to *Creative Writing and the New Humanities*, Paul Dawson writes: "Within [creative writing], the literary work can be conceptualized as a zone of social contestation not by dismantling the desire to craft an individual work of art, or by policing the literary representation of identity in the service of social justice, but *by exploring how the compositional process is a mode of social intervention at the level of discourse*. By doing this writers can be seen as public intellectuals, not in the nostalgic sense of independent freelance thinkers, but as participants in the intellectual work of the New Humanities (214, emphasis mine)." I would argue that to "explore the compositional process [as] a mode of social intervention" requires not only acknowledging, naming, and framing the ways in which the digital inflects the process of crafting an imaginary text—as I have done throughout this book—but also the deep and long-term examination of what it means to frame creative writing this way (i.e., the social intervention). How must the field of creative writing wield its understanding of the technologies that enable as much as limit the writer's work? And how is the emerging networked discipline of the digital humanities poised to consider what it means for nonhermeneutic approaches that employ and examine "practices of (imaginative) making?"

These two questions form a horizon line for creative writing studies. On the one end we can see that creative writing studies will continue to develop its own disciplinary identity. On the other we can see that creative writing studies will also take on the project of thinking interdisciplinarily—thinking with the digital humanities so that it can speak back to it—to develop nonhermeneutic approaches toward the study of technologically mediated making. New kinds of authority, new ideological perspectives, new student subjectivities, new genres, and new processes, as this book shows, surface as the first few major terms to help us navigate what it means to study composition and creative writing in the digital humanities. As creative writing and composition studies continue to evolve alongside the digital humanities, we must point these sets of conditions toward that horizon. The degree to which we will be able to see writing thrive through yet another technological and cultural paradigm shift—from print to digital—depends upon how clearly we are willing to see that horizon approaching.

Works Cited

Aldridge, John W. *Talents and Technicians: Literary Chic and the New Assembly-line Fiction*. New York: Scribner, 1992. Print.

Arthur, W. Brian. *The Nature of Technology: What it is and How it Evolves*. New York: Free Press, 2009. Print.

Baxter, Charles. *Burning Down the House: Essays on Fiction*. Saint Paul: Graywolf Press, 1997. Print.

Bennet, Eric. *Workshops of Empire: Stegner, Engle, and American Creative Writing During the Cold War*. Iowa City: University of Iowa Press, 2015. Print.

Berlin, James. "Rhetoric and Ideology in the Writing Class." *College English* 50 (1988): 477–94. Print.

Berlin, James. *Rhetoric and Reality: Writing Instruction in American Colleges, 1900-1985*. Carbondale: Southern Illinois University Press, 1987. Print.

Berlin, James. *Rhetorics, Poetics, and Cultures: Refiguring College English Studies*. Urbana: NCTE, 1996. Print.

Berry, David, ed. *Understanding Digital Humanities*. New York: Palgrave Macmillan, 2012. Print.

Berthoff, Ann. "From Problem-solving to a Theory of Imagination." *College English* 33 (1972): 636–49. Print.

Bishop, Wendy. *Colors of a Different Horse: Rethinking Creative Writing Theory and Pedagogy*. Urbana: NCTE, 1994. Print.

Bishop, Wendy, ed. *Elements of Alternate Style: Essays on Writing and Revision*. New York: Heinemann, 1997. Print.

Bishop, Wendy. "Places to Stand: The Reflective Writer-Teacher-Writer in Composition." *College Composition and Communication* 51.2 (1999): 9–31. Print.

Bizzaro, Patrick. "Research and Reflection in English Studies: The Special Case of Creative Writing." *College English* 66.3 (2004): 294–309. Print.

Bizzaro, Patrick. "Writers Wanted: A Reconsideration of Wendy Bishop." *College English* 71 (2009): 256–70. Print.

Bloom, Lynn. *Composition Studies as a Creative Art: Teaching, Writing, Scholarship, Administration*. Logan: Utah State University Press, 1998. Print.

Brooke, Collin. *Lingua Fracta: Towards a Rhetoric of New Media*. Cresskill: Hampton Press, Inc., 2009. Print.

Burdick, Anne, Johanna Drucker, Peter Lunenfeld, Todd Presner, and Jeffrey Schnapp, eds. *Digital_Humanities*. Cambridge, MA: The MIT Press, 2012.

Cain, Mary Ann. "'To Be Lived': Theorizing Influence in Creative Writing." *College English* 71.3 (2009): 217–28. Print.

Clark, Michael Dean, Trent Hergenrader, and Joseph Rein. *Creative Writing in the Digital Age*. London: Bloomsbury, 2015. Print.

Coover, Robert. "The End of Books." *Colors of a Different Horse: Rethinking Creative Writing Theory and Pedagogy*, edited by Wendy Bishop and Hans Ostrom, 257–66. Urbana: NCTE, 1994. Print.

Danielewski, Mark Z. *House of Leaves*. New York: Pantheon Books, 2000. Print.

Dawson, Paul. *Creative Writing and the New Humanities*. London: Routledge, 2005. Print.

Donnelly, Dianne, ed. *Does the Writing Workshop Still Work?* Bristol: Multilingual Matters, 2010. Print.

Donnelly, Dianne. *Establishing Creative Writing as an Academic Discipline*. Bristol: Multilingual Matters, 2012. Print.

Egan, Jennifer. "Black Box." *The New Yorker*. Web. June 2, 2012. http://www.newyorker.com/online/blogs/books/2012/06/jennifer-egan-black-box.

Elbow, Peter. *Writing Without Teachers*. Oxford: Oxford University Press, 1998. Print.

Emerson, Lori. *Reading Writing Interfaces: From the Digital to the Book Bound*. Minneapolis: University of Minnesota Press, 2014. Print.

English Department. George Mason University. Web July 24, 2012. http://english.gmu.edu/course_sections?code=ENGH&term=201270.

Eshun, Kodwu. *More Brilliant Than the Sun: Adventures in Sonic Fiction*. London: Quartet Books, 1998. Print.

Faigley, Lester. *Fragments of Rationality: Postermodernity and the Subject of Composition*. Pittsburgh: University of Pittsburgh Press, 1992. Print.

Franzen, Jonathan. *The Kraus Project*. New York: Farrar, Straus, and Giroux, 2013. Print.

Funkhouser, C. T. *New Directions in Digital Poetry*. London: Bloomsbury, 2012. Print.

Funkhouser, C. T. *Prehistoric Digital Poetry: An Archeology of Forms*. Tuscaloosa: The University of Alabama Press, 2007. Print.

Glaser, Jennifer and Laura R. Micciche. "Digitizing English." *Rhetoric and the Digital Humanities*. Chicago: University of Chicago Press, 2015. Print.

Glazier, Loss Pequeno. *Digital Poetics: The Making of E-Poetries*. Tuscaloosa: The University of Alabama Press, 2002. Print.

Gold, Matthew, ed. *Debates in the Digital Humanities*. Minneapolis: University of Minnesota Press, 2012. Print.

Goldsmith, Kenneth. *Uncreative Writing*. New York: Columbia University Press, 2011. Print.

Gopnick, Adam, ed. *Best American Essays 2008*. New York: Mariner, 2008. Print.

Haake, Katherine. "Re-envisioning the Workshop: Hybrid Classrooms, Hybrid Texts." In *Does the Writing Workshop Still Work?*, edited by Dianne Donnelly, 182–94. Bristol: Multilingual Matters, 2010. Print.

Haake, Katherine. *What Our Speech Disrupts: Feminism and Creative Writing Studies*. NCTE, 2000. Print.

Harman, Graham. *Tool-Being: Heidegger and the Metaphysics of Objects*. Chicago: Open Court Press, 2002. Print.

Harper, Graeme and Jerri Kroll. *Creative Writing Studies: Practice, Research, and Pedagogy*. Clevedon: Multilingual Matter, 2008. Print.

Hawk, Byron. *A Counter-History of Composition: Towards Methodolgies of Complexity*. Pittsburgh: University of Pittsburgh Press, 2007. Print.

Hayles, N. Katherine. *Writing Machines*. Cambridge: The MIT Press, 2002. Print.

Heidegger, Martin. *Being and Time*. Translated by John Macquarrie and Edward Robinson. New York: Harper and Row, 1962. Print.

Heidegger, Martin. *Poetry, Language, Thought*. Translated by Albery Hofstadter. New York: Harper and Row, 1971. Print.

Hergenrader, Trent, Michael Clark, and Joseph Rein. *Creative Writing in the Digital Age*. London: Bloomsbury, 2015. Print.

Hesse, Douglas. "The Place of Creative Writing in Composition." *College Composition and Communication* 62.1 (September 2010): 31–37. Print.

Howard, Rebecca Moore. "A Plagiarism Pentimento." *Journal of Teaching Writing*. 11.3 (Summer 1993): 233–46. Print.

Kac, Eduardo, ed. *Media Poetry: An International Anthology*. Chicago: University of Chicago Press, 2010. Print.

Katz, Stephen. *The Epistemic Music of Rhetoric: Toward the Temporal Dimension of Affect in Reader Response and Writing*. Carbondale: Southern Illinois University Press, 1996. Print.

Kirschenbaum, Matthew G. "What is Digital Humanities and What's It Doing in English Departments?" *ADE Bulletin* 150 (2010): 1–7. Print.

Landow, George. *Hypertext 3.0: Critical Theory and New Media*. Baltimore: The Johns Hopkins University Press, 2006. Print.

Lethem, Jonathan. "The Ecstasy of Influence: A Plagiarism." *Harper's Magazine*. February 2007. Web. July 24, 2012. http://harpers.org/archive/2007.

Letter, Amy. "Creative Writing for New Media." In *Creative Writing in the Digital Age*, edited by Trent Hergenrader, Michael Clark, and Joseph Rein, 177–90. London: Bloomsbury, 2015.

Macrorie, Ken. *Telling Writing*. New York: Heinemann, 1985. Print.

Macrorie, Ken. *Uptaught*. New York: Boynton/Cook, 1970. Print.

Massumi, Brian. *Parables for the Virtual*. Durham and London: Duke University Press, 2002. Print.

Mayers, Tim. "Creative Writing and Process Pedagogy." *Creative Writing Pedagogy for the Twenty-first Century*. Carbondale: Southern Illinois University Press, 2015. Print.

Mayers, Tim. "One Simple Word: From Creative Writing to Creative Writing Studies." *College English*, 71.3 (2009): 217–28. Print.

Mayers, Tim. *(Re)writing Craft: Composition, Creative Writing, and the Future of English Studies*. Pittsburgh: University of Pittsburgh Press, 2005. Print.

McGurl, Mark. *The Program Era: Postwar Fiction and the Rise of Creative Writing*. Cambridge: Harvard University Press, 2011. Print.

McLuhan, Marshall. *Understanding Media: The Extension of Man*. Cambridge, MA: The MIT Press, 1964. Print.

Miller, Paul D. *Rhythm Science*. Cambridge: Mediawork/The MIT Press, 2004. Print.

Miller, Susan. "Writing Studies as a Mode of Inquiry." In *Rhetoric and Composition as Intellectual Work*, edited by Gary A. Olson, 41–54. Carbondale: Southern Illinois University Press, 2002. Print.

Monson, Ander. *Vanishing Point: Not a Memoir*. Minneapolis: Graywolf Press, 2010. Print.

Monson, Ander. Vanishing Point: A Book and a Website by Ander Monson. Web. July 12, 2012. http://otherelectricities.com.

Moody, Rick. "Some Contemporary Characters." *Electric Literature 3*. February 23, 2010. Web. June 2, 2012.

Morton, Donald and Mas'ud Zavarzadeh. "The Cultural Politics of the Fiction Workshop." *Cultural Critique* 11 (Winter 1988): 155–73. Print.

Moxley, Joseph. *Creative Writing in America: Theory and Pedagogy*. Urbana: NCTE, 1989. Print.

Myers, D. G. *The Elephants Teach: Creative Writing Since 1880*. New York: Prentice Hall, 1995. Print.

North, Stephen. *The Making of Knowledge in Composition: Portrait of an Emerging Field*. Montclair: Boynton/Cook, 1987. Print.

Olson, Gary. "The Death of Composition as an Intellectual Discipline." *Composition Studies* 28.2 (Fall 2000): 33–41. Print.

Olson, Gary. *Rhetoric and Composition as Intellectual Work*. Carbondale: Southern Illinois University Press, 2002. Print.

Ong, Walter. *Orality and Literacy: The Technologizing of the Word*. New York: Routledge, 1982. Print.

Ong, Walter. "Writing is a Technology that Restructures Thought." *Literacy: A Critical Sourcebook*, edited by Ellen Cushman, Eugene R. Kintgen, Barry M. Kroll, and Mike Rose, 19–31. Boston: St. Martin's, 2001. Print.

Owens, Derek. *Resisting Writings (and the Boundaries of Composition)*. Dallas: Southern Methodist University Press, 1994. Print.

Peary, Alexandria and Tom C. Hunley. *Creative Writing Pedagogies for the Twenty-first Century*. Carbondale: Southern Illinois Press, 2015. Print.

Perlhoff, Marjorie. *Radical Artifice: Writing Poetry in the Age of Media*. Chicago: University of Chicago Press, 1991. Print.

Reid, Alexander. *The Two Virtuals: New Media and Composition*. Lafayette: Parlor, 2007. Print.

Rettberg, Scott. "Electronic Literature as Digital Humanities." In *Blackwell Companion to Digital Humanities*, edited by Susan Schreibman, Ray Siemans, and John Unsworth, 127–36. New York: Wiley-Blackwell, 2008. Print.

Ricardo, Francisco, ed. *Literary Art in Digital Performance*. London: Bloomsbury, 2009. Print.

Rice, Jeff. "The Making of Ka-Knowledge: Digital Aurality." *Computers and Composition* 23 (2006): 266–79.

Rice, Jeff. *The Rhetoric of Cool: Composition Studies and New Media*. Carbondale: Southern Illinois University Press, 2007. Print.

Rice, Jeff. "Occupying the Digital Humanities." *College English* 75 (2013): 357–78. Print.

Rickert, Thomas. "Language's Duality and the Rhetorical Problem of Music." In *Rhetorical Agendas: Political, Ethical, Spiritual*, edited by Patricia Bizzell, 157–63. Mahwah, NJ: Lawrence Erlbaum, 2006. Print.

"Rick Moody's Novel Experiment with Microserialization." Future Perfect Publishing, November 30, 2009. Web. July 24, 2012. http://futureperfectpublishing. com/2009/11/30/rick-moodys-novel-experiment-with-microserialization/.

Ritter, Kelly. "Professional Writers/Writing Professionals: Revamping Teacher Training in Creative Writing PhD Programs." *College English*, 64.2 (2001): 205–27. Print.

Ritter, Kelly and Stephanie Vanderslice. *Can it Really Be Taught? Resisting Lore in Creative Writing Pedagogy*. New York: Heinemann, 2007. Print.

Schreibman, Susan, Ray Siemans, and John Unsworth, eds. *Blackwell Companion to Digital Humanities*. New York: Wiley-Blackwell, 2008. Print.

Selfe, Cynthia. "Technology and Literacy: A Story About the Perils of Not Paying Attention." *The Norton Book of Composition Studies*. W. W. Norton and Company, 2009. Print.

Shields, David. *Reality Hunger: A Manifesto*. New York: Vintage, 2011. Print.

Shipka, Jody. *Toward A Composition Made Whole*. Pittsburgh: University of Pittsburgh Press, 2011. Print.

Sirc, Geoffrey. *English Composition as a Happening*. Logan: University of Utah Press, 2002. Print.

Starkey, Dave, ed. *Teaching Writing Creatively*. New York: Heinemann, 1998.

Sullivan, Patricia Suzanne. *Experimental Writing in Composition: Aesthetics and Pedagogies*. Pittsburgh: University of Pittsburgh Press, 2012. Print.

Tate, Gary, Amy Rupiper, and Kurt Schick. *A Guide to Composition Pedagogies*. Oxford: Oxford University Press, 2001. Print.

The Writing Program. University of Massachusetts – Amhurt, 2009. Web. July 24, 2012. http://www.umass.edu/writingprogram/geninfo/experimental.html.

Tobin, Lad and Thomas Newkirk. *Taking Stock: The Writing Process Movement in the 90s*. Portsmouth, NH: Boynton/Cook, 1994. Print.

Trimbur, John. "Changing the Question: Should Writing Be Studied?" *Composition Studies* 31.1 (Spring 2003): 15–24. Print.

Trimbur, John. "Literacy and the Discourse of Crisis." *The Politics of Writing Instruction: Postsecondary*, edited by Richard Bullock and John Trimbur, 277–95. Portsmouth, NH: Boynton/Cook, 1991. Print.

Ulmer, Gregory. *Internet Invention: From Literacy to Electracy*. New York: Longman, 2003. Print.

Ulmer, Gregory. *Heuretics: The Logic of Invention*. Baltimore: Johns Hopkins University Press, 1994. Print.

Vickers, Brian. "Figures of Rhetoric/Figures of Music?" *Rhetorica: A Journal of the History of Rhetoric* 2.1 (1984): 1–44. Print.

Wilkinson, Alec. "Something Borrowed." *The New Yorker*. October 5, 2015. Print.

Williams, Bronwyn T. "Digital Technologies and Creative Writing Pedagogy." *Creative Writing Pedagogies for the Twenty-first Century*. Carbondale: Southern Illinois University Press, 2015. Print.

Winterowd, W. Ross. *The English Department: A Personal and Institutional History*. Carbondale: Southern Illinois University Press, 1998. Print.

Wittig, Rob and Mark C. Marino. "Acting Out: Netprov in the Classroom." *Creative Writing in the Digital Age*, edited by Trent Hergenrader, Michael Clark, and Joseph Rein, 153–64. London: Bloomsbury, 2015. Print.

Wysocki, Anne, Johndan Johnson-Eilola, Cynthia L. Selfe, and Geoffrey Sirc. *Writing New Media: Theory and Applications for Expanding the Teaching of Composition*. Logan: Utah State University Press, 2004. Print.

York, Jake Adam. "Let Stones Speak: New Media Remediation in the Poetry Writing Classroom." *Creative Writing Studies: Practice, Research, and Pedagogy*. Clevedon: Multilingual Matter, 2008. Print.

Index

"Acting Out: Netprov in the Classroom"   129
"Advanced Composition" courses   7
aesthetics, and creative writing   2–6
"Afternoon, A Story"   9, 50
The Alliance of Digital Humanities Organizations   14
The Art of Fiction (Gardner)   108
Association of Writing Programs (AWP)   47
authorship   49, 51, 60–3, 66, 123
AWP. See Association of Writing Programs (AWP)

Barthes, Roland   56, 134
Baxter, Charles   96–8, 100–5, 109–10
Bazerman, Charles   14
Beastie Boys   89
Bell, Madison Smartt   108
Belsey, Catherine   85–6
Benjamin, Walter   60
Berlin, James   20, 34, 92
Bernstein, Charles   135
Berry, David   14
Berthoff, Ann   23–8, 33–4, 42
The Best American Essays 2008   58–9
Bishop, Wendy   1, 7–8, 16, 26, 29, 37–9, 48, 52, 119–21, 123–4, 126
Bizzaro, Patrick   1, 7, 26, 37, 39, 45, 48
"Black Box"   59, 110
Blackwell Companion to Digital Humanities   14
Bloom, Lynn   37–8, 120
The Body of Michael Brown (poem)   81, 85
Bradbury, Ray   72
Brooke, Collin   5
Brooks, Cleanth   108
Brown, Jim   127
Brown, Michael   81–2, 84–5
Burdick, Anne   14
Burroughs, William   60, 72
Byrne, Mairéad   81

Cain, Mary Ann   45
Can It Really Be Taught? Resisting Lore in Creative Writing Pedagogy (Ritter and Vanderslice)   8, 39
Carver, Raymond   69
categorical systems, and creative writing   12–15
CCCC. See Conference on College Composition and Communication (CCCC)
"Changing the Question: Should Writing Be Studied?"   119
Chen, Ken   82
Clark, Michael   16
collaborative creative space   10
College Composition and Communication (Harris)   6, 119
College English   23, 39, 45, 49, 67, 134
Colors of a Different Horse (Bishop and Ostrom)   8, 16, 52
composition. See also creative writing; digital humanities (DH)
   and creative writing   6–9
   creativity in   23–6
   critical-creative   13, 29–35
   and imaginative texts   1, 10–11, 16, 18, 41, 43, 45, 47, 50, 56–7, 62, 66–7, 72, 77, 83, 90, 92, 95, 100, 103, 113–15, 117, 125–6, 130, 132, 136–7
   invention and imagination in   26–9
   and new media   35–40
Composition Studies as a Creative Art (Bloom)   38
Computers and Composition   5, 15, 36
concretists   72
Conference on College Composition and Communication (CCCC)   4, 35, 37
context-is-the-new-content approach   61
Cooper, Douglas   50
Coover, Robert   16, 52–3, 125
A Counter-History of Composition (Hawk)   5

craft criticism   13, 19, 41–2, 46–50, 54, 57–9, 62–3, 65–7, 76, 95–6, 103, 111–12, 117
creative composition. *See* creative writing
creative nonfiction   57
creative writing. *See also* composition; digital humanities (DH)
   aesthetics and   2–6
   authors, institutions, and ideology   60–5, 91–3
   and authorship   49, 51, 60–3, 66, 123
   and categorical systems   12–15
   and composition   6–9
   craft and contours   66–7
   and craft criticism   46–50
   and cultural conditions   96–103
   and digital humanities   40–3
   and disciplinary identity   131–4
   and electromagnetic imaginary   96–103
   and electronic ethos   80–5
   and freedom   69–70
   and genres   57–60, 112–17
   and hypertext   50–7
   and knowledge production   112–17
   and landscape as canvas   85–91
   medial ecologies and subject positions   77–9
   and media software   36, 52, 82, 89, 128–30
   mediated writer's subjectivity   79–80
   methodologies   123–7
   and pedagogy   127–31
   and process   112–17
   and rhythm science   85–91
   and technology   9–11
   as technology   103–11
   texts and tweets   71–5
   voice and unoriginality   75–7
"Creative Writing and Process Pedagogy"   95, 114
Creative Writing and the New Humanities (Dawson)   45, 75, 132, 137
"Creative Writing for New Media"   74, 128
Creative Writing in America (Moxley)   8, 121
Creative Writing in the Digital Age (Hergenrader, Clark and Rein)   16, 132

Creative Writing Pedagogies for the Twenty-first Century (Peary, Hunley and Williams)   7, 128, 132
Creative Writing Studies: Practice, Research, and Pedagogy (Harper and Kroll)   128
critical-creative composition   13, 19, 29–35
Critical Practice (Belsey)   85
cultural conditions, and creative writing   96–103
"The Cultural Politics of the Fiction Workshop"   69
cyberfeminism   51, 126

Danielewski, Mark Z.   54–5, 103
Dartmouth Conference   23, 28, 32, 36
Dawson, Paul   1, 45, 74–6, 132, 137
Debates in the Digital Humanities (Gold)   14
Debord, Guy   72
Delirium (Cooper)   50
DH. *See* digital humanities (DH)
Dick, Philip K.   72
digital craft criticism   13, 19, 41–2, 46–50, 54, 57–9, 62–3, 65–7, 76, 95–6, 103, 111–12, 117
Digital_Humanities (Burdick, Drucker, Lunenfeld, Presner and Schnapp)   14
digital humanities (DH). *See also* composition; creative writing
   and creative writing   40–3
   and fenceless neighbors   134–8
   methodological   123–7
   new wave of   15
   and pedagogy   127–31
Digital Humanities Quarterly   14
digital multimodality   2, 6, 13, 53, 56, 74, 88, 102, 113
"digital natives"   64
Digital Poetics: The Making of E-Poetries (Glazier)   9
digital processes, and creative writing   50–7
Digital Storytelling *(The Writing Program)*   64
Digital Studies   14
"Digital Technologies and Creative Writing Pedagogy"   113

"Digitizing English" 133
disciplinary identity, and creative
    writing 131–4
DJing 87, 91, 109
DJ Spooky 87, 89, 102, 109
Does the Writing Workshop Still Work?
    (Donnelly) 8, 45
Donnelly, Dianne 1, 8, 45, 64,
    123–4, 131
double consciousness 86
Drucker, Johanna 14
Du Bois, W. E. B. 86
Dworkin, Craig 135

"The Ecstasy of Influence: A
    Plagiarism" 60
Egan, Jennifer 20, 59, 73, 110–11
Elbow, Peter 3, 19, 29–31, 38, 84, 120
electracy 5
Electric Literature 59
electromagnetic imaginary, and creative
    writing 96–103
electronic ethos, and creative
    writing 80–5
"Electronic Literature as Digital
    Humanities" 114
Electronic Poetry Center 135
Elements of Alternate Style
    (Bishop) 37–8
*The Elephants Teach: Creative Writing Since
    1885* (Myers) 7, 39
Emerson, Lori 10
"The End of Books" 16, 52
"Engfish" 29–30
English Composition as a Happening
    (Sirc) 2, 31, 36
Enlightenment 83, 92
Eshun, Kodwo 55, 102
*Establishing Creative Writing Studies an
    Academic Discipline* (Mayers and
    Donnelly) 64, 123, 131
"Experimental Writing Workshop" 64
expressive discourse 27–8, 33
expressive realism 86, 88

Facebook 71
Faigley, Lester 20, 74, 83–5, 89
Fenza, D. W. 47–8
"Florida School" 5

*Fragments of Rationality: Postmodernity
    and the Subject of Composition*
    (Faigley) 83, 85
Franzen, Jonathan 20, 97–105, 107–10,
    116–17
freedom, and creative writing 69–70
Frey, James 62–3
"From Problemsolving to a Theory of the
    Imagination" 23
Funkhouser, C. T. 9
Future Perfect Publishing 59
Futurrhythmachinic Discontinuum 55

Gardner, John 108
generative codes 92
generative syntaxes 109–10
genres, and creative writing 57–60,
    112–17
Glaser, Jennifer 133, 135, 137
Glazier, Loss Pequeno 9
Gold, Matthew 14
Goldsmith, Kenneth 16, 19, 50, 60–3, 65,
    70, 72–4, 76–8, 80–2, 84–5, 87, 90–1,
    102, 112–13, 125, 135
Gordon, Caroline 108
A Guide to Composition Pedagogies (Rupier,
    Schick and Tate) 7

Haake, Katharine 1, 7–8, 37, 39, 46, 48
Harman, Graham 106
Harper, Graeme 1, 2, 128
Harris, Joe 119
Haunted 55
Hawk, Byron 5, 15
Hayles, Katherine 53–5, 62, 74, 77–8, 80,
    87, 91
Heidegger, Martin 20, 41–3, 103,
    105–10
Heine, Heinrich 97, 99
Hergenrader, Trent 16
Hesse, Douglas 1, 6–7, 15, 17
The House of Fiction (Gordon and
    Tate) 108
House of Leaves (Danielewski) 54–5
Hunley, Tom C. 7
hypertext, and creative writing 9, 50–7
*Hypertext 3.0: Critical Theory and New
    Media* (Landow) 52
Hypertext Fiction Workshop 125

imagination, in composition   26–29
imaginative texts   1, 10–11, 16, 18, 41, 43,
    45, 47, 50, 56–7, 62, 66–7, 72, 77,
    83, 90, 92, 95, 100, 103, 113–15, 117,
    125–6, 130, 132, 136–7
Inanimate Alice (Pullinger and
    Joseph)   55–6, 127
information sickness   97
institutional conventional wisdom   40, 47
institutionality, and creative
    writing   60–5, 91–3
Internet   73, 112
invention, in composition   26–9
Iowa Writers Workshop   12
iStories   73–4

Jackson, Shelly   50–2, 126
Johnson-Eilola, Johndan   4, 15
Jorn, Asger   72
Joseph, Chris   55, 127
*A Journal of Rhetoric, Writing, and
    Culture*   5
Joyce, James   60, 72
Joyce, Michael   50

Kac, Eduardo   9
Kairos   5, 15, 36, 50, 54
ka-knowledge   88–9
Kameen, Paul   1, 7
Kaye cipher   77–8, 80, 87
Keywords in Creative Writing (Bishop and
    Starkey)   8, 39
Kirschenbaum, Matthew   14
knowledge production, and creative
    writing   112–17
Koh, Adeline   14, 127
Kraus, Karl   97–9, 101, 109
The Kraus Project (Franzen)   20, 97, 116
Kroll, Jeri   2, 128, 132

Landow, George   9, 52–3, 56
Leroy, J. T.   62–3
Lethem, Jonathan   60, 62–3, 103
Letter, Amy   74, 128–9
Lin, Tao   71
Lingua Fracta (Brooke)   5
Literary Art in Digital Performance
    (Ricardo)   66
literary realism   70, 72
Lunenfeld, Peter   14

McGurl, Mark   39, 108
McLuhan, Marshal   59, 111, 117
Macrorie, Ken   3–4, 19, 29–31, 34, 38, 84
"The Making of Ka-Knowledge: Digital
    Aurality"   88
*The Making of Knowledge in Composition:
    Portrait of an Emerging Field*
    (North)   27
Marino, Mark C.   129
Mason, George   64
Massumi, Brian   56
Mayers, Tim   1, 7–8, 12, 19, 20, 26,
    39–42, 45–9, 67, 76, 95–6, 107,
    114, 123
medial ecologies and subject
    positions   53, 77–9
Media Poetry: An International Anthology
    (Funkhouser)   9
media software, and creative writing   36,
    52, 82, 89, 128–30
mediated writer's subjectivity   79–80
methodological digital humanities   123–7
MFA programs   54, 63–4, 84
Micciche, Laura R.   133, 135, 137
Miller, Paul   20, 86–92, 102–3, 105,
    109–10, 117, 135
Miller, Susan   20, 123, 136
Mingus, Charles   86
Monson, Ander   11, 57–60, 62, 73, 80, 87,
    103, 110, 112, 126
Moody, Rick   11, 20, 59, 73, 110
*More Brilliant Than the Sun: Adventures in
    Sonic Fiction* (Eshun)   55
Morton, Donald   69–70, 72, 74–7, 79,
    84–5, 90
Moxley, Joseph   8, 121–2
multimodality   2, 6, 13, 53, 56, 74, 88,
    102, 113
multiplex consciousness   86
Murray, Donald   84, 120
Myers, D. G.   7–8, 39

Nabokov, Vladimir   72
Narrative Design (Bell)   108
Narrative Magazine   73
"The Navidson Record"   54
Nestroy, Johann   97
"netprov"   11, 129
New Directions in Digital Poetry
    (Funkhouser)   9

New Humanities   137
new media, and composition   35–40
New Media Poetics: Contexts,
    Technotexts, and Theories
    (Funkhouser)   9
The New Yorker   59, 81, 110
North, Stephen   27
Notorious B.I.G.   89

"Occupying the Digital Humanities"   134
Olson, Gary   120–3
"One Simple Word: From Creative
    Writing to Creative Writing
    Studies"   45, 67
Ong, Walter   20, 103, 105–9
Ostrom, Hans   8, 16, 48, 52
Owens, Derek   2, 19, 25, 30–4, 38

Parables for the Virtual (Massumi)   56
Patchwork Girl   50–2, 126
Payano, Beverly   97
Peary, Alexandria   7
pedagogy, and digital humanities   127–31
PennSound   135
Perloff, Marjorie   81–2
Phaedrus (Plato)   104
The Pinch   58
"The Place of Creative Writing in
    Composition"   6, 8
"Places to Stand: The Reflective
    Writer-Teacher-Writer in
    Composition"   119
plagiarism   60
Plato   104, 105
practices of making   133, 135, 137
Prehistoric Digital Poetry: An Archeology of
    Forms (Funkhouser)   9
Prensky, Marc   64
Presner, Todd   14
print culture   72–4
process, and creative writing   112–17
"Professional Writers/Writing
    Professionals: Revamping Teacher
    Training in Creative Writing PhD
    Programs"   65
The Program Era: Postwar Fiction and
    the Rise of Creative Writing
    (McGurl)   39, 108
proto-expressionism   92
Pullinger, Kate   55, 127

"The Question Concerning
    Technology"   105

reading/writing   49, 69, 72, 74, 77–80, 86,
    90. *See also* creative writing
Reading Writing Interfaces: From
    the Digital to the Book Bound
    (Emerson)   10
read-write system   56
Reality Hunger: A Manifesto (Shield)   62
Reid, Alexander   5
Rein, Joseph   16
Reitter, Paul   99
Released into Language (Bishop)   123
"Research and Reflection in English
    Studies: The Special Case of Creative
    Writing"   39
Resistant Writings (and the Boundaries of
    Composition) (Owens)   2, 30–1
Rettberg, Scott   114–16
(Re)Writing Craft (Mayers)   8, 39–40,
    47–8, 76
Rhetoric and Composition as Intellectual
    Work (Olson)   123
Rhetoric and Reality (Berlin)   34, 92
The Rhetoric of Cool: Composition Studies
    and New Media (Rice)   5, 36, 53,
    60, 116
Rhetorics, Poetics, and Cultures
    (Berlin)   92
Rhythm Science (Miller)   86, 91, 102, 109
Ricardo, Francisco   66
Rice, Jeff   5, 15, 36–7, 43, 53, 58, 60,
    88–91, 116, 134–5, 137
Ritter, Kelly   1, 7–8, 37, 39, 45, 65
River City. See The Pinch
Rose, Mike   120
The Rumpus   97
Rupiper, Amy   7
Rushdie, Salman   99

Schick, Kurt   7
Schnapp, Jeffrey   14
Schramm, Wilbur   108
Selfe, Cynthia   4, 35–6, 42–3
sensualism   99
Seventh Letter   104
Shields, David   11, 62–3
Shipka, Jody   13, 15, 73–4
Short, Emily   11

Sirc, Geoffrey   2, 4, 19, 25, 31–2, 34, 36, 38
Socrates   104
"Solipsism"   58
"Some Contemporary Characters"   11,
      59, 110
"Something Borrowed" event   81
spiritualism   99
standing-reserves   42–3, 106
Starkey, Dave   37, 39
Stein, Gertrude   60, 72
stillness   96–7, 100
StorySpace   36, 52
The Story Workshop (Schramm)   108
student-centered writing program   29
student subjectivity   77–9
Sullivan, Patricia Suzanne   5, 38

Talking Back (Hooks)   83
Tate, Allen   108
Tate, Gary   7
Teaching Writing Creatively (Starkey)   39
technology
      and creative writing   9–11, 103–11
      and electromagnetic
            imaginary   96–103
      essence of   105–7, 110
      -fueled postidentity writing
            practice   80
Telling Writing (Macrorie)   3, 29
Tinderbox   52
"To Be Lived: Theorizing Influence in
      Creative Writing"   45
Tobin, Lad   28, 120
*Tool-Being: Heidegger and the Metaphysics
      of Objects* (Harman)   106
Toward a Composition Made Whole
      (Shipka)   13, 73
"Traffic" (poem)   61
transformative pedagogy   28
Trimbur, John   119, 121, 126
Truant, Johnny   54
Twitter   11, 59, 73, 99, 110
The Two Virtuals (Reid)   5

Ulmer, Gregory   5, 15
U-Mass-Amherst's Experimental Writing
      Workshop   125
Uncreative Writing   61

Uncreative Writing class   112, 125
Uncreative Writing (Goldsmith)   16, 60,
      62, 65, 70, 72, 76, 80, 85, 102
Understanding Digital Humanities
      (Berry)   14
Understanding Fiction (Brooks and
      Warren)   108
Understanding Media (McLuhan)   59, 111
Uptaught (Macrorie)   30

Vanderslice, Stephanie   1, 7–8, 37, 39, 45
Vanishing Point (Monson)   57–8, 73, 80,
      110, 126
A Visit From the Goon Squad   59
voice, and unoriginality   75–7

Warhol, Andy   60, 62, 72
Warren, Robert Penn   108
web 2.0 technologies   52, 54
*What Our Speech Disrupts: Feminism and
      Creative Writing Studies* (Haake)   8,
      39, 48
Wilkinson, Alec   81–2
Williams, Bronwyn T.   113–14, 128
Winterowd, W. Ross   29
Wittig, Rob   129
workshop poetics   75
Writer's Chronicle   47
"Writers Wanted: Reconsidering Wendy
      Bishop"   45
"Writing is a Technology that Restructures
      Thought"   103
Writing Machines (Hayles)   53–4, 77
*Writing New Media: Theory and
      Applications for Expanding the
      Teaching of Composition* (Wysocki
      and Johnson-Eilola)   4
"Writing Studies"   136
"Writing with Machines: Data and Process
      in Taroko Gorge"   127
Writing Without Teachers (Elbow)   29–30
Wysocki, Anne   4

Yancey, Kathleen Blake   15, 120
York, Jake Adam   128–9

Zavarzadeh, Mas'ud   69–70, 72, 74–7, 79,
      84–5, 90

CPSIA information can be obtained
at www.ICGtesting.com
Printed in the USA
LVHW010420240821
695911LV00006B/539